PRAISE FOR *MAXIMIZE YOUR SOCIAL*

"Neal Schaffer is one of the few true expert strategists in this vast new social media reality we live in."

—**Pepe Aguilar**
Eight-time Grammy-winning artist;
President of Green Dream Social

"Neal Schaffer is one smart cookie. So take a bite out of his new book, *Maximize Your Social*. And while you're chewing, rework your social media strategy!"

—**Brian Carter**
Author of the international best-seller *The Like Economy:*
How Businesses Make Money with Facebook

"Neal Schaffer understands that social media and marketing were not invented in a vacuum, and that if we bring to our understanding of the communications revolution many of our former skills and ideas about business, we can actually succeed at this new game with a minimum of trauma."

—**Robin Carey**
CEO, Social Media Today

"As a fellow Forbes Influencer, I've had the opportunity to watch Neal's acumen in action. In this new book he brings the social media message to large organizations, and gives today's busy executives the tools they need to embrace social media. After you read his book, you'll understand where the ROI is, and how to sell it."

—**Marsha Collier**
Author of *The Ultimate Online Customer Service Guide:*
How to Connect with Your Customers to Sell More

"Neal is one of the smartest social media marketers on the planet. His ability to combine technical expertise with a holistic approach to social is what really makes him a standout. Every time I get the chance to speak with him I learn something new. Oh, and he's a hell of a nice guy."

—**Jason Miller**
Senior Social Media Strategist, Marketo

"Building on his unique background in international business development and marketing, Neal provides a strong strategic perspective combined with a practical step-by-step approach to social media."

—**Kathy Simmons**
CEO, NETSHARE, Inc./Experts Connection

"Neal Schaffer is an outstanding speaker, consultant, and educator in the social media marketing arena. He brings years of practical business experience to a subject that is often misperceived as child's play. He approaches the topic and use of social media with a creative and solutions-driven approach that cuts through the hype with a focus rarely seen in this space. Neal has taught hundreds of executives at Rutgers

Center for Management Development how to develop strategic and tactical social media marketing initiatives to achieve business challenges. He leverages principles that avoid shiny object syndrome and maintains flexibility in a dynamic space."

—**Peter Methot**
Director of Marketing and Program Development,
Rutgers Center for Management Development

"Social media is revolutionizing the way brands interact with customers, and practitioners such as Neal Schaffer are at the forefront of communicating what that change means for business—where to get started and how to capitalize on the opportunity. In this book, Schaffer provides no-nonsense advice on determining your social media objectives, developing a strategy, making the most of your content, engaging your customer base, and managing the risks. More important, he also outlines where to identify the ROI on your social efforts and how to communicate success to the rest of the business. Schaffer writes like he presents—in a practical, anecdote-filled way that is easy to relate to your own experiences. If you want to understand how social is moving from being a pure marketing tool to being a medium that can and should be used throughout your entire organization, then read this book."

—**Richard Owen**
CEO, MeetTheBoss TV

"Social media is vexing for a lot of marketers because it is different from traditional and web channels. If you're looking for a framework for framing how social media should be integrated into your overall marketing strategy, this is the resource you need."

—**Chris Treadaway**
CEO, Polygraph Media

"An indispensable guide for navigating the rapidly changing world of content marketing and social media. By making optimal use of the big four—Facebook, Twitter, LinkedIn, and Google+—and being prepared for new platforms that may be just around the corner, Neal Schaffer's insights are invaluable for nonprofit organizations."

—**Anthony Flint**
Fellow and Director of Public Affairs, Lincoln Institute of Land Policy

"Neal Schaffer's new book *Maximize Your Social* is must-read for any business executive or owner to better understand why they need to embrace social media as an integrated part of the company's marketing mix. Neal's delivery style is approachable, engaging, and (most important) actionable. Neal demonstrates how an effective social media strategy is a must-have for any company to win in today's marketplace."

—**Glenn Gaudet**
President and Founder, GaggleAMP

"Now that everyone can have a voice if they choose to, Schaffer explains the ins and outs of social media and the steps to be taken in order to create a social media strategy. This book provides a practical guide on how to leverage your voice to its full advantage. It's a must for anyone who is responsible for developing a social media plan."

—**Arnie Kuenn**
President, Vertical Measures

"If you're ready to get past the basics, then Neal Schaffer's *Maximize Your Social* is everything you're looking for. Neal is one of the nation's leading experts, and he's put together a step-by-step guide that shows you how to get past the fundamentals and create a goal-oriented, metrics-based social media program."

—**Jamie Turner**
CEO, 60SecondMarketer.com

"Neal is the most connected guy I know. He's literally friends with everyone I've met in the social media marketing world—but not 'friends' in a passive sense, like so many of us on social media are. No, Neal is an active friend. He listens, he advises, he coaches, he helps spread the word, and he gives feedback. And that's exactly the kind of guy from whom you want to receive advice on social media strategy. Neal doesn't just know social media strategy—he lives it. So if you want to jump right into what it feels like to have Neal Schaffer as an active friend, then read this book. And when your social media accounts start flourishing as a result of Neal's advice, go friend him on Facebook and say thanks."

—**Joshua Parkinson**
Founder, PostPlanner

"To succeed in today's world, you must learn to navigate and leverage social media and its enormous potential to bring you closer to your fans and customers. In his latest book, Neal Schaffer will show you how. Whether you're just getting started in social media or you want to take your social media efforts to the next level, *Maximize Your Social* orients you to the new environment and guides you to maximize your social. A must-read for everyone, from the new social media manager to CEOs."

—**Eric Kim**
Founder and CEO, Twylah

"Neal Schaffer became an invaluable source of strategic guidance for 1World Online advising on how to extract true value from social media and convert them into tools for our service growth. *Maximize Your Social* will now allow every company to tap into his truly unique expertise in understanding this new business reality of—and how to best leverage—social media."

—**Alex Fedosseev**
CEO, 1WorldOnline

"*Maximize Your Social* is a must-read for any business looking to reach out, engage, and get measurable results from marketing on social media."

—**Tammy Kahn Fennell**
CEO, MarketMeSuite

"We've reached a point in the social media revolution in which organizations need to mature beyond an ad hoc approach. In *Maximizing Your Social,* Neal Schaffer has written a welcome and comprehensive strategic approach that includes a drill-down to tactics for the major social media platforms. This is a must-read for entrepreneurs and social media professionals alike."

—**Ric Dragon**
Author of *Social Marketology*

"*Maximize Your Social* draws on Neal's breadth of client experience to give insights into actionable strategy and tactical tips to flourish and avoid social media failure. Having worked with Neal on B2B social media strategy, I know this book brings real-world insights—not only into client acquisition and retention through social media, but also into the mechanics and operational challenges you and your organization will face."

—**Nick Allen**
Digital Strategist

"Stop waiting for an outside expert to come in with a cookie-cutter plan; you know your company and its business objectives best. This book gives you the confidence to understand the landscape of social media marketing and quickly turn your insights into a playbook that you can begin using right away."

—**Liz Philips**
Social Media Manager, TaylorMade Golf

MAXIMIZE

YOUR

SOCIAL

A ONE-STOP GUIDE TO BUILDING A SOCIAL MEDIA STRATEGY FOR MARKETING AND BUSINESS SUCCESS

NEAL SCHAFFER

WILEY

For general information about our other products and services, please contact our Customer Care Department within the United States at (800) 762-2974, outside the United States at (317) 572-3993, or fax (317) 572-4002.

Wiley publishes in a variety of print and electronic formats and by print-on-demand. Some material included with standard print versions of this book may not be included in e-books or in print-on-demand. If this book refers to media such as a CD or DVD that is not included in the version you purchased, you may download this material at http://booksupport.wiley.com. For more information about Wiley products, visit www.wiley.com.

Library of Congress Cataloging-in-Publication Data:

Schaffer, Neal.
    Maximize Your Social: A One-Stop Guide to Building a Social Media Strategy for Marketing and Business Success/Neal Schaffer.
        pages   cm.
    Includes index.
    ISBN: 978-1-118-65118-6 (cloth); ISBN: 978-1-118-75663-8 (ebk);
    ISBN: 978-1-118-75668-3 (ebk)
        1. Branding (Marketing)   2. Customer relations.   3. Social media.   4. Information technology—Management.   I. Title.
    HF5415.1255.S393   2013
    658.8'72—dc23

                                                            2013019100

Printed in the United States of America

10 9 8 7 6 5 4 3 2 1

Contents

Introduction

Whenever I present on social media in front of a business audience, I always explain what my professional background was before the advent of Facebook, Twitter, LinkedIn, and other social platforms. You, like the members of my audience, should ask the same of anyone who is trying to offer advice on how your business can use social media. The reason is simple: the professional experience we had before the emergence of social media deeply affects the way we look at how businesses can and should leverage the new opportunities social media provides us. A search engine optimization expert will have a very different perspective than someone who is well versed in public relations. Equally, a "traditional" digital marketer will probably have a completely different perspective than someone with a background in corporate communications.

In the same manner, before we dive into the practical aspects of this book, I want to give you a snapshot of my own professional experience and how it shapes the advice I am about to provide you.

My professional experience has been in business-to-business (B2B, a term I will often refer to throughout this book) sales, business development, and marketing. I should point out that the first 15 years of my career were spent living in Asia and helping foreign businesses launch new sales organizations from scratch and successfully develop new business thereafter. Similar to the way in which learning Mandarin Chinese greatly helped me gain fluency in Japanese, launching a sales operation from scratch in China for a multibillion-dollar Japanese semiconductor company helped me successfully launch the Western Japan sales office for an American-embedded software company, as well as generate revenues equivalent to more than a quarter of global business from scratch in just two years for a Canadian-embedded software company.

With each business challenge that I accepted, I was representing a company with little or no brand awareness in foreign territory—with the additional challenge that I needed to help market these brands using a foreign language! This experience required me to holistically analyze foreign business environments while working within many areas of the companies and developing practical solutions to help our sales and marketing efforts. There were no role models to mirror, because most foreign companies were not successful at the time, and the ones that were had been built upon historical brand awareness.

In essence, I was creating and implementing a complete corporate strategy for how these companies could launch new business, and I not only was often in charge of the final sales and profit numbers but also had to handle non-sales-related and non-marketing-related issues, such as human resources, customer support, legal, administration, and even information technology (IT).

In addition, I had to be a translator, not only to market products and services from a foreign client in a foreign country, but also to report back to my foreign headquarters regarding what we could do to quickly close current opportunities as well as generate a robust pipeline for the future.

For many businesses, social media is a similarly foreign land. Traditional methods of communication, based on either rigid web copy "script" or language used in advertising that was intended for one-way communication from the brand to the audience, are the reason why some social media crises are born and develop viral legs. Companies with branding guidelines have trouble finding what language they are going to use in the diverse world of social media. How do you create a voice for your company that both aligns with your brand equity and satisfies the requirements of social media users? After all, social media was created for people, not companies, so what should companies talk about in a room full of people?

Of course, social media is not a singular entity: each social media site differs in terms of its history, culture, and functionality. Your average

Facebook user would find it odd if you used a hashtag in your post (although Facebook has recently introduced this functionality), whereas many LinkedIn users would be taken aback if you post updates to your network that are overtly personal. I argue that, just as you would never market a product or service the exact same way to China, Japan, and Korea, you would never speak the same language in the similarly diverse communities of Facebook, Twitter, and LinkedIn.

I don't know if my unique background has provided me with an equally unique insight or not, but I do strongly believe that this experience—in addition to my professional experience in consulting, speaking, training, and coaching companies of all sizes, from start-ups to Fortune 500 companies, on how best to maximize social media—has provided me with enough background to help your company look at social media in a new way. Your company will need as holistic of a social media strategy as I had to create for each unique business environment I encountered in Asia.

A recent industry report that surveyed more than 3,000 marketers indicated that 83 percent of marketers wanted help in creating a social media strategy,[1] and that is the primary focus of the book from which we will begin. However, more than 83 percent of the same marketers also wanted to understand which social tactics were most effective, what are the best ways to engage an audience via social media, and how to measure their return on investment from their social media activities. All of these crucial topics will be covered in this book, which is structured as follows:

- Chapter 1 will get you up to speed on your understanding of recent trends in the business use of social media, regardless of how little or how much experience you have had until now. To get the most out of this book, this will be critical for you to understand.
- Chapters 2 through 5 will then go on to help you create your social media strategy, including helping you determine your social media business objectives as well as assisting you in auditing your current social media efforts.
- Chapters 6 through 11 will provide targeted tactical advice on the major platforms that will appear in most social media strategies: blogging, Facebook, Twitter, LinkedIn, Google+, and the visual social networks of YouTube, Pinterest, and Instagram.

- Chapters 12 through 17 will then look at the company-wide issues that will undoubtedly arise as you implement your social media strategy. It is here where the question of the return on investment of your social media strategy will be covered in depth.

By following the advice in this book of creating a strategic framework, leveraging the strategic opportunities that each social media channel offers, and implementing a data-driven approach to monitor the success, or failure, of your social media program, your brand or business will also be able to leverage the potential that social media has—and thus truly "maximize your social."

Chapter 1   Reality Check

The Permeating Trends of Social Media and Social Business

Whether you're just getting started with social media, revamping your current efforts through the creation of a social media strategy, or wanting to see what ideas I have to help you propel your social media to a new level, it is important to take a step back and make sure we all equally understand the current trends—and therefore potential scale—that social media holds for all businesses. Just as those who attend my speaking events have varying levels of social media experience, I assume the readers of this book range from beginners to experts. Given that the understanding and experience of using social media for business is different from reader to reader, I like to make sure we all start from the same place when discussing the topic of social media.

I like to discuss three main themes when doing so:

1. Convergence of information and communication
2. Social media's permeation of industry and corporate discipline
3. Big social data and the accessibility of public information

CONVERGENCE OF INFORMATION AND COMMUNICATION

Let's make one thing clear: social media was made for people, not for businesses. Representing a brand, your challenge is to engage with others in a medium that was originally created for people to keep in touch with one another. Fortunately, we have seen a shift in the way that people use social networking sites. Today, more social media users are using the communication tools provided by social media websites to seek out information for their professional and private use.

As someone who remembers life before the Internet, contrasting today with life then provides an interesting picture of this new world that we live in and its potential for businesses. In the past, we all had equal access to a limited amount of information that was spoon-fed to us from a finite number of news sources. Because of this, not only was how we all consumed information limited, but we all shared much commonality in what news we read. The media outlets were able to capitalize on this fact (and still do) by charging a great deal to be able to advertise through these limited outlets, which held huge listening, viewing, and reading audiences captive. In terms of communication with one another way back in the day, we used snail mail or the good old landline telephone.

The digital age, which began with the advent of the Internet and the advance of wireless technologies, allowed both our media consumption as well as our communication to become digital. Channels for both media consumption and communication increased, but the lines between personal communication and media consumption were still separate.

Enter social media. Although most of us joined social networking channels to connect with old classmates (Facebook) or colleagues (LinkedIn), the way we use these same networking sites has been transformed over the past few years. When looking at our News Feed, perhaps we find a link to a Facebook page offering a discount or a news update that interests us. Soon we begin to find—and consume—more information within social media without even doing searches on Google. For some of us, sites such as Twitter, news sources such as LinkedIn Today, or communities such as LinkedIn Groups become our go-to places to look for the latest information on breaking news or whatever interests us.

One of the first instances where this convergence of information and communication became clear was when a US Airways plane made a successful emergency landing on the Hudson River on January 15, 2009. On that day, "[Twitter] user Janis Krums was aboard a ferry used to rescue stranded passengers, and uploaded the news-breaking photo[1] to TwitPic from his iPhone during the rescue. His caption read 'There's a plane in the Hudson. I'm on the ferry going to pick up the people. Crazy.'"[2] This photo announced the news of the crash on Twitter first—10 minutes after takeoff—although the story did not "break" on the *New York Times* site until 16 minutes after the picture was uploaded.[3]

Sites that were meant for social networking have now become the channels where the news breaks. Information and communication are happening simultaneously in social media. This convergence has accelerated to the point where a Skype-like mobile application for private communication popular in Japan called LINE, which has more than 100 million users, recently allowed brands to create accounts and message users[4]; users receive a notification on their smartphones as if it was coming from a friend. Even the Securities and Exchange Commission (SEC) now allows companies to announce key information in compliance with Regulation Fair Disclosure on social media outlets such as Facebook and Twitter.[5]

What does all this mean? I believe that this convergence of information and communication provides all businesses the following three distinct opportunities:

1. **Reach out and engage with customers, prospects, partners, and your network**. Social media provides equal opportunities to engage with current customers in a new and exciting way and to engage and reach out to potential new ones. Although social customer relationship management (CRM) software is still in development, savvy salespeople are already using social media ad hoc to network with and reach out to those who might become future customers. If you consider social media a 24/7 virtual online networking world, you see the opportunities in doing

everything online that you are used to doing for your company offline. Keep in mind that if you are not engaging with your clients in social media, your competitors might already be doing so!

2. **Create opportunity by communicating and sharing information.** If many professionals and consumers are looking for—or finding—information in various social media channels, your company should have a presence there and be providing your company's content to these interested parties. Obviously, social media is not about self-promotion only, so information that is shared should go beyond just your own company's blog. There is no *TV Guide* for the Internet (or social media), so you'll want to share enough relevant content with your particular target demographic that your social media account becomes the channel to which they tune. This means you need to talk about more than just your company, and this may involve curating third-party content as well as crowdsourcing content from your fans.

3. **Manage your reputation and discover new business through monitoring information.** Although it's obviously a best practice to be listening to all the social media conversations around you as part of your social media strategy, monitoring social media feeds is equally important for big and small companies. Companies that have invested a great deal in their brand equity are sometimes in a defensive mind set when it comes to social media monitoring, working to capture negative tweets and proactively manage them before a social media crisis erupts. On the other hand, businesses also use social media to monitor conversations in hopes of generating new leads or finding new product ideas.

SOCIAL MEDIA'S PERMEATION OF INDUSTRY AND CORPORATE DISCIPLINE

I have worked as a social media consultant, speaker, trainer, and coach for dozens of organizations. These entities range from business-to-consumer companies to those in niche industries that sell to only other businesses. I've also worked with nonprofits, educational institutions, and think tanks. The message from this experience is clear: there is no industry that cannot—and should not—maximize the potential that social media offers.

I often challenge attendees of my speaking events to name an industry in which social media has no relevance. Back at a speaking event in 2010, one woman representing a public utility expressed that she couldn't see how on earth her company could be using social media. Interestingly enough, over the past few years many public utilities have embraced social media, some reactively after being hit by a crisis that forced it to become very active in social media to win back the public's trust and repair its damaged reputation.

Another example of social media use in this industry comes from one of my recent consulting clients. This client decided to proactively ramp up its social media presence to build goodwill to help offset any potential social media crisis it might face in the future. This same public utility client also showcases how far social media has come from being a pure marketing tool to being a medium that can and should be used throughout your company. Although the sponsor for my project was in the marketing communications department, I asked that every internal department that had a stake in the company's social media approach be brought to the table for our first meeting, which was an internal hearing on the company's use of social media. Needless to say, the room was filled with representatives from practically every department.

A look at how a platform such as Twitter could be used throughout a company provides an easy-to-understand example of how social media is beginning to permeate departments' use of social media in almost every industry imaginable. Companies usually have members of their public relations, corporate communications, or marketing departments man their Twitter accounts. Over time, companies realize they need to have corporate governance of social media policies (managed by legal departments) as well as the creation and implementation of social media guidelines (managed by human resources). If salespeople want to utilize social media to better engage with their clients, someone from information technology (IT) is called in to decide on the best tools to use, as well as potentially integrate social media functionality into the corporate website. Of course, it will take only one complaint about a product or service to get customer service involved, which may require a dedicated Twitter account for those purposes. Internal hiring managers might also see Twitter emerging as a potential social recruiting platform.

In such a way, social media has evolved from an inside-out promotional medium to an outside-in conversation taking place with the public where conversations happening throughout social media affect the way that some companies do business. This is how I would best define the evolution from social media to something I would call social business, a buzzword that we often hear in social media circles these days. Your understanding of this evolution will help you create a social media strategy with your entire company in mind, which will be beneficial for your business in the long run.

BIG SOCIAL DATA AND THE ACCESSIBILITY OF PUBLIC INFORMATION

There is a lot of talk in the IT world about big data. A growing amount of this big data comes from the world of social media in the form of uploaded videos, photos, podcasts, blog posts, status updates, discussions, and messages. Although much of big social data is hidden behind privacy settings that limit public access to them, there is a growing amount of data that is publically available for businesses to analyze and learn from. Imagine having the ability to see and evaluate conversations among customers, competitors, and prospects going on around the world and utilizing those data to predict future consumption trends. That world has already begun.

Although many on Facebook or LinkedIn might not make their conversations accessible to the public beyond their own friends or network, a platform such as Twitter is an example of a social network where an overwhelming majority of conversations are available for public consumption. In fact, the US Library of Congress has been archiving our Tweets for some time now. Likewise, although Google+ allows users to share information privately within circles, there are plenty of public conversations on display.

Harnessing all this information is no easy feat, and those who are analyzing it are using listening platforms such as Radian6 or Sysomos to data mine, aggregate, and make sense of it. A friend of mine who is in charge of social media for a beverage company mentioned how the company could analyze public information to look for hints of what new flavors of coffee or tea to develop. The company could also see what topics were being discussed vis-à-vis coffee and tea in regions they already serve and, based on share of voice, determine how well its regional distributors were doing.

Companies have always had the ability to harness the power of their customers' voices to improve their products. Windows 7 is an example of a product that was driven by the error reports and feedback provided by Vista users. Now businesses large and small can actually use a much larger data set to glean insight that can be utilized for new product research, competitive analysis, and even prediction of future needs.

Although the three trends mentioned in this chapter may seem futuristic to your business, your understanding of their potential will greatly help you in both the creation and implementation of your social media strategy. It's now time to start working on how your particular business should be approaching the ever-changing and evolving world of social media.

Chapter 2   A Social Media Strategy

The Framework for the Ever-Changing World of Social Media

Although I agree with Peter Drucker's statement that "culture eats strategy for breakfast,"[1] managing social media for your business has such a huge potential to eat up precious hours of your employees' time and span across several departments that there is a need to create and manage internal processes. Furthermore, you need to know how well your social media program is doing and what other things you could be doing to maximize your social. This is why, although organic and spontaneous social media activities might work at some companies with the right culture, most businesses require a road map to provide structure to manage their social media programs over time.

WHY IS THERE A NEED FOR A SOCIAL MEDIA STRATEGY?

A social media strategy is the only rational response to the need for collaboratively creating a written piece that all internal parties can agree on. It can determine how many resources are used for what social media activity as well as define what tactics you will and won't pursue in social media. It serves as your road map for the present and future, and should personnel change, it still carries on its main function.

Most important, creating a robust social media strategy is the secret to managing your social media return on investment (ROI). Because creating any strategy begins with determining your company's specific objective, this book will help you create a social media strategy that will allow you to create metrics to assess whether or not you achieved a positive social media ROI. It will also help you optimize your strategy to further increase your ROI.

A concise social media strategy with well-defined objectives, tactics, and metrics is the only rational solution to help you manage and make sense of all the social media activities in which your staff engages. No longer will you have to question how well you're doing in social media; on the contrary, once you have a social media strategy, you'll be wondering what more you can be doing to maximize your business success from your social media efforts!

THE EVER-CHANGING SPECTRUM OF SOCIAL MEDIA

There's another critical reason why every business needs a social media strategy: social media is always changing.

Clients often want to know what's next in social media. Most companies haven't fully maximized the potential that the existing social networks offer, so instead of looking into the future, I recommend that clients stay in the here-and-now.

The problem with the present state of social media, though, is that it is always in flux. To predict the future of social media, we need to look at its past and see just how transformed these platforms have become as they have been hijacked by people and businesses for utilization that was simply not conceived at their inception:

Facebook began as a social networking site strictly for college students and now has a user base where 57 percent of the Facebook population is aged 35 or older.[2]

Twitter was originally created as a short messaging service to communicate with a small group of people over mobile phones.[3] Now Twitter is literally where the news breaks, as indicated in incidents like the aforementioned US Airways emergency landing, as well as more recent events such as the death of Whitney Houston, where it was reported on Twitter 27 minutes before it was announced by the press.[4] LinkedIn began as a social networking site for professionals, beginning with the five founders sending out invitations to 350 of their friends.[5] Now it is the default site for both job seekers to announce that they're looking for a job as well as for headhunters and corporate recruiters to find them. When looking at the past of social media, there is an interesting trend that bubbles to the surface and best explains why social media has always been—and will always be—in flux:

- The users of each social media channel are always changing.
- The way we use each social media website is ever changing.
- The functionality provided by each site is constantly in flux.

With so much flexibility within social media, strategies and tactics that you used yesterday may not be as effective today. Furthermore, a one-time strategy without review and optimization may hide opportunities in new and emerging social networking sites such as Google+, Pinterest, or Instagram. In other words, a social media strategy can help you understand where to focus your efforts and optimize your tactics and, if managed properly and regularly, can help future-proof social media efforts regardless of change.

In the ever-changing spectrum of social media, those organizations without a social media strategy are operating blindly or haphazardly. Those with a social media strategy and regular review of their metrics can both understand how well they are doing and optimize accordingly, regardless of future changes to existing networks or the emergence of new ones.

PDCA: A LOGICAL FRAMEWORK FOR SOCIAL MEDIA STRATEGY CREATION

If social media is beginning to sound like one big experiment, you're right; that's exactly what it is. In fact, if you think of social media as an experiment, you'll begin to appreciate the logical framework I think is as effective in social media management as it is for the controlled lab experiments that it could have been designed for: the Deming, or PDCA, cycle.

The Deming cycle is named after its founder, W. Edwards Deming, said to be the father of modern quality control[6] and whose contributions to Japanese manufacturing and business have given him a hero status in that country.[7] I can say from personal experience working at a semiconductor manufacturer in Japan that mid-level employees underwent internal training on the concept of PDCA and how to apply it to their own work. This is an important concept in Japan, and it is the best framework I can find for a social media strategy. PDCA is extremely simple and eloquent in concept:

P stands for plan, which is, in essence, the social media strategy that you will create.

D stands for do, which is the implementation of your social media strategy according to plan.

C stands for check, which means analyzing the key performance indicators (KPIs) and metrics regarding your social media and seeing how they performed when compared with the assumptions in your social media strategy.

A stands for act, but it could also mean adjust, meaning that based on the results from step C, you optimize your P and repeat the cycle.

The cycle, as you can imagine, is never ending, because the eternal flux of people and social media means you will never be operating at optimal performance. Only by constantly planning, implementing, checking, and optimizing will your business achieve excellence in social media, regardless of what your specific corporate objectives might be.

THE ESSENTIAL COMPONENTS IN ANY SOCIAL MEDIA STRATEGY

Chapter 5 of this book deals with the detailed sections that will be included as part of your social media strategy, but now that I've mentioned PDCA, I want you to begin thinking about these essential components of any social media strategy and what your company's

P will need to incorporate (these will be covered in more depth in Chapter 3):

- **Objective:** This is the reason for the existence of your social media strategy. Without a clearly defined objective, you'll never be able to create clearly defined KPIs that will allow you to measure your ROI. Ideally, this objective should align with your corporate strategy, because your social media program should be an integral part of your business.
- **Customer:** Who is your target customer? The more detailed demographic details you know about the type of people with whom you want to engage, the better you can align your social media activities with them. Understanding what makes your target audience tick and why they use social media will become essential to the successful implementation of your social media strategy.
- **Share:** If social media is about the convergence of communication and information, what on earth is your business going to share with social media users? If you work in a business-to-business (B2B) company, this will often come down to content that you might already be sharing with your current and prospective clients on sales calls, in newsletters, or during informative webinars. If you work for a company that sells directly to consumers, it might mean sharing more photos and videos of who is using your product or the many ways in which it can be used, stories about your brand that have never been publicly discussed, or resourceful information to nudge people into realizing they need your product.
- **Who:** It's one thing to write a social media strategy, but it's even more important to decide who is going to implement the strategy on your behalf: Will it be an internal employee, or will the work be outsourced to an agency? One of the benefits of creating your own social media strategy is that it's easy to outsource it because the tactics of what an agency should implement are well defined in the strategic plan. That being said and all things being equal, your company's social media presence is a reflection of your brand; therefore I recommend that every company that has the resources to implement its social media strategy in-house use its present employees.
- **Brand:** Most businesses already have brand guidelines, and these should be applied to your social media properties as well. After all, branding

is all about consistency, right? The challenge, though, is that most branding guidelines don't include any guidance for the most important part of your brand in social media conversations: *your voice*. Although your brand guidelines might make mention of tone and vocabulary for use in web copy, social media will challenge those guidelines when you need to have a conversation with an average person.

Now that you have started thinking about the background for your social media strategy, it's time to begin its creation by determining your starting point: your objective(s).

Chapter 3   Determining Objectives and Background for Your Social Media Program

The creation of any social media strategy starts with soul searching vis-à-vis determining your objective or what you want to achieve through your social media program. Once the objective is decided, the first step is to flesh out other areas concerning your target demographic group, market focus, and branding guidelines, because the remainder of your strategy will be leveraging these. This chapter will explain how to create each section in order to prepare a comprehensive foundation for your strategy. Main points included in this section should be included in an executive summary, which would ideally precede this background information.

A holistic approach should be taken in determining the basis for your social media strategy. Ideally, the mission in creating and implementing your social media strategy should highlight the potential that social media has in merging with legacy marketing and communication activities as well as cross-organizational roles to reach specific strategic objectives that exist regardless of social media.

BUSINESS OBJECTIVES AND PROJECTED OUTCOMES

Business objectives and projected outcomes require complete clarity in what you are trying to achieve in social media and, if successful, what the outcome would look like. Determining your objective cannot be overemphasized; this is how you'll you determine success for your social media strategy—and therefore how you judge the return on investment (ROI) of your social media program.

I encourage my customers, as I would encourage you, to start with your current corporate strategy. Perhaps you have an annual strategy, a three- to five-year strategy, or both. Look at each of the key points in your strategy and see where a social media presence might help you achieve or accelerate the achievement of specific corporate objectives. If you are unclear as to what is achievable in social media for each social media channel, your industry, or a specific department in your company, make sure you skim through my Maximize Social Business blog at http://maximizesocialbusiness.com and read my overviews of maximizing each of the social media channels in Chapters 6 through 11 before actually proceeding with the creation of your social media strategy.

If you don't have any place to start—and you want to align your social media strategy objectives with clearly defined ROI metrics—you might want to consider these objectives tied to specific bottom-line numbers:

Increase Sales

- Develop new business for new clients or new products.
- Improve your customer retention rate and increase sales to current clients.
- Increase your brand awareness in the market.

Decrease Expenses

- Use social media to recruit new employees or add to your talent pipeline.

- If your customers are using social media and asking questions or requesting support through their tweets to you, consider shifting some of your customer support resources to manage a customer support–related social media channel. This will potentially decrease customer expenses by providing more efficient support through this new platform.
- Shift some of your marketing budget to social media and see if you can achieve more with social media than you did with traditional marketing activities. Common areas that are decreased to make room for social media include traditional media advertising, search engine optimization, and pay-per-click (PPC) advertising budgets.

Still looking for other potential objectives that you might want to consider for your social media strategy? Here are some ideas derived from my past experience. These cover the different ways companies from all industries of all sizes utilize social media:

- Establish an infrastructure to govern internal social media efforts going forward.
- Generate new business for your established company or a new brand or product line within your existing company.
- Generate more traffic to either your website or your brick-and-mortar store.
- For some start-up companies, especially in e-commerce, use social media as your primary marketing channel.
- Build a greater social media audience or nurture a large social media community as part of your corporate marketing and communications infrastructure.
- Scale usage of social media internally as an organization.
- Integrate social media into your current digital properties.
- Engage customers wherever they are, realizing that social media is a viable and needed new communication platform.
- Attract more business from your current customers by engaging with them via social media.
- Further extend your brand into the social media communities of your customers to improve public goodwill.
- Attract social media influencers in order to better amplify your social media messages.

- Attain thought leadership in your industry through social media engagement.
- Provide distributors, resellers, and other partners with social media content they can reuse for their own social efforts.
- Proactively approach social media in preparation for an inevitable crisis and understand what to do in terms of crisis management from a social media perspective.

Based on the objective or combination of objectives that you determine for your social media strategy, the projected outcomes might already be set in stone. For instance, the establishment of an infrastructure to oversee the implementation of your strategic plan can in itself be a projected outcome. Further projected outcomes from almost any social media strategy include greater reach in social media channels, more conversations with social media users who will help extend your public goodwill into social media communities and increase your thought leadership, and increased traffic to your website.

As for other projected outcomes, they should be based on the metrics that prove whether or not you reached each specific objective. It should be noted that although the strategic approach outlined in this book will help increase the effectiveness of your efforts, social media is a time-intensive resource. The ROI of your social media efforts will be covered in depth in Chapter 17, but note that any projected outcomes are purely bound by the strategic effort applied in implementing your social strategy to its fullest.

TARGET DEMOGRAPHIC GROUP

The target demographic group for your social media strategy should be based not only on who your current or potential customer is but also on whom among them is using which social media channels and in what way. The more details you know about your target customers, the easier it will be for you to decide on the content and channel strategy for a social media program.

If you're trying to figure out who your target demographic is, there are some easy ways to do this:

- Generate a survey for your current clients and ask them for demographic information in exchange for providing them with something of value.

- Manually research information available on public websites, including social media, about a sampling of your customers. Use this information to draw a larger picture about them.
- Use the demographic details available from your web analytics program (for example, Google Analytics).
- Analyze the demographics of your current social media followers through Facebook Insights or LinkedIn Company Analytics (or LinkedIn Group Statistics if your company manages one).
- Advertise to your competitors' fans. If Facebook will be one of your targeted social media channels—and you already have a competitor who has a strong presence there—you can use Facebook advertising to see what demographic will be enticed to click on your ads (see Chapter 7 for more details). Note the same is true of using LinkedIn Ads if your competitor has a LinkedIn Group (see Chapter 9 for more details).
- Analyze the demographics of your competitors' web presence. Although there is no one ideal tool to use for this, there are a number of tools that you can use to help get a picture of the type of people visiting your competitors' or your own website. These include Compete,[1] Alexa,[2] and Google Ad Planner.[3]

At a minimum, when considering your target demographic group, you should try to ascertain the following information, which you can ideally glean from your current customer base (or estimate who you think your new customers will be if your main social media strategy objective is in developing new business):

- Gender
- Age
- Language(s) spoken
- Location
- Education
- Profession
- Interests (related and not related to your product)
- Media consumed (Where do they go online/offline for information?)
- Social media channels most active on

If you're having trouble creating one target demographic group or if your demographic group varies from product to product or industry to industry, pick the leading demographic characteristic on which to base your social media strategy. In the future, you can include other demographic characteristics and target them in a strategic way as part of a phased approach to your social strategy.

TARGET MARKET FOCUS

Although the target demographic section of your social media strategy should focus on the detailed specifics regarding your target customer in a micro fashion, the section on target market focus should look at potential markets that you want to engage with from a macro level. For instance, are you purely targeting the consumer market or business-to-business market? Are you targeting certain industries or regions of the country or world? Perhaps your focus is a combination of the above.

Similar to the target demographic focus, your first social media strategy ideally should concentrate on only one strategic market. After all, part of a strategy is deciding what *not* to focus on. Once you feel comfortable in the strategic implementation of your social media program for one target market, it will be easier to either widen your approach for additional markets or supplement your current strategy with additional instructions to optimize your strategy for other markets.

BRANDING GUIDELINES

Just as your social media strategy should be aligned with your overall corporate strategy, the branding guidelines for your social media strategy should be aligned with your overall corporate branding guidelines. Normally, your branding guidelines might be contained in one document or separated into design guidelines for visual aspects and an editorial style guide for the written word. Although social media is a new, more conversational channel, the same branding guidelines should apply; remember, the cornerstone of corporate branding is consistency across channels.

Unfortunately, although aligning your branding guidelines to the guidelines in these existing corporate documents to the fullest extent possible is recommended, they will undoubtedly fall short or need to be modified in certain aspects. Some of these areas might include:

- **Tone of voice:** With the exception of YouTube videos and photos and illustrations, the written word might become the primary focus of your social media activities. The tone outlined in many corporate branding guidelines might be too neutral for social media. To increase engagement in certain conversational social media channels, such as Facebook, using a more conversational voice might be worth considering based on engagement metrics from individual posts. You should also be cognizant of your target demographic group and ensure that the voice you use in social media is aligned with their expectations.

- **Imagery:** The use of imagery, specifically photography and illustration, should be a part of any strategic plan, because it is an effective way to engage with social media users. Regardless of whether you decide to use visual social media channels such as Pinterest or Instagram for your strategy, images are useful at a minimum for blogs (as eye candy) and for Facebook (as an engagement vehicle). Make sure your current guidelines for imagery take this into account; if they don't, create an addendum to address this.

- **Video:** Some branding guidelines address video only as static content that lives within the private walls of a corporate website. A social media strategy uses video as an embeddable technology—one that is primarily uploaded to YouTube with no limit on time display other than the current restrictions that YouTube has. Note that at the time of this writing, YouTube allows all users to upload videos as long as 15 minutes apiece, but there is a way to request YouTube to upload longer videos.[4]

- **Social media:** If you're lucky, your current branding guidelines will have some recommendations already built in regarding social media. However, for most companies, recommendations likely cover the bare minimum in terms of establishing the visual components for brand pages on various social media channels (for example, cover logo usage, background image for social media channels, and potentially language and tone). Any branding guidelines that you create anew for this social media strategy should be augmented to your current corporate branding guidelines.

Now that we've fully developed the foundation of our social media strategy, it's essential to conduct a social media audit before filling in the details of the overarching strategy.

Chapter 4   Auditing Your Social Media Program

Just as listening before engaging in social media is important, there are many who augment the PDCA Deming cycle by preceding it with an O for observation. Others have called this step "grasp the current condition."[1] An audit should not be solely about your own social media channels but rather about all your digital properties and marketing channels. As mentioned repeatedly in this book, your social media program should not exist within a silo in your company and it should be integrated with all your outward-facing properties and efforts. Furthermore, the notion of an audit should also be spread out to include the social media presence of competitors. By doing so, you might be able to find a role model to help guide your business in the social media journey, especially if you are a relative latecomer to using social media.

EXISTING DIGITAL PROPERTIES AND MARKETING CHANNELS

Let's first take a look at your current existing digital properties and marketing channels to understand how social media might be better integrated with them. Note that we will cover social media integration in more depth in Chapter 16.

Assuming that your company is an established business, you probably already have a number of existing marketing channels, in both traditional and digital spaces, that should be considered when deciding how social media can best be integrated with their presence:

- A **website** can be fully integrated with social media.
- **Newsletters** can be integrated with social media.
- Any **content** created for outlets outside of your own digital properties can be repurposed and used as part of your social media strategy, including potentially adding links in your social media channels to your byline, should you have one.
- **Events** of all types can be integrated with your social media efforts in many exciting ways.
- **Pay-per-click (PPC) ads** (paid advertisements that appear in search results) that have been used on Google can also be used on social media websites to microtarget certain demographic groups for brand awareness and campaigns.
- **Traditional print, radio, and television ads** can be integrated with social media simply by including them as icons or optionally adding your social media URLs or strategic hashtags next to or in lieu of the icons.

While taking an inventory of your current digital properties as part of your audit for this social media strategy, make note of the different channels that can and should be fully integrated with the social media strategy plan that you are creating.

SOCIAL MEDIA AUDIT

A social media audit based on your brand's current presence is essential to create baseline metrics for your own social media strategy and to determine how you compare with your competitors. The baseline metrics that are created as part of your social media audit will also help in creating the industry role models covered later in this chapter.

Although there are many things you can audit, I like to base social media audits on publicly available data so that comparisons with your competitors will not be limited by insufficient information. For this reason, I recommend that you audit the following metrics:

- **Customer base/market share:** Obviously, if you have public information regarding customer base/market share and can compare it with your competitors', it may help explain the differences in metrics you see when making a comparative analysis of your social media presence.
- **Website rank:** Assuming a blog is an integral part of your social media strategy, hopefully you'll see an overall increase in your website traffic after implementing your social media strategy, regardless of your objective. Although you can use website analytics such as Google Analytics to get detailed website traffic information regarding your own blog, it is impossible to do so for your competitors'. For this reason, while not perfect, Alexa is a service that can be referenced for this metric.
- **Reach:** Conceding that Facebook fans and Twitter followers can be bought, both through fake fan providing services as well as through opting in via social ads, the number of fans/followers is still a sign of potential reach in that particular social media channel and becomes a baseline metric for your internal use as well as when comparing yourself against competitors. You should be auditing the following platforms and numbers:
    o Blog RSS subscribers
    o Facebook fans
    o Twitter followers
    o LinkedIn company page followers
    o LinkedIn Group members
    o Google+ brand page circlers
    o Google+ Community members
    o YouTube channel subscribers
    o Pinterest followers
    o Instagram followers

- **Frequency:** How often are you posting on each of your social media channels? This includes both proactive posting as well as reactive engagement. Pick a defined period of time (week, month, quarter, etc.) and calculate the number of times you have posted to each channel. After an audit, many companies find that the amount of posting they do on each platform is completely out of balance with the prioritization they committed to in their social media channel strategy. This is the first step in ascertaining whether or not your company is making the same mistake.

- **Engagement:** What is the interaction between your social media posts and your fans? Although publicly available and easy to calculate, metrics limit what we can measure here. Following are some easy metrics to use for your audit and for comparisons of your program with your competitors':

  o Blog: How many comments are you getting per post? How many social shares on which platforms are you getting per post? I personally place more value on the social share as a metric for content amplification and engagement.[2]

  o Facebook (PTAT/fans): For any given fan page, Facebook provides us with the number of likes as well as the "people talking about this" (PTAT) number, an indication of how many News Feed stories a page's fans are creating as a result of engaging with the page. Although the PTAT number is showing the figure from the prior seven days and thus is a changing metric, it is a good metric to watch regarding what percentage of fans are engaging with a page.

  o Twitter: How many @ mentions is your brand receiving? How many retweets is your content getting on average? If you are active on Twitter, you'll definitely want to limit your data sampling. I recommend using Twitter.com to gather this data to ensure it is accurate and straight from the source. You can grab competitor data in a similar manner.

  o LinkedIn: How many likes and comments does each company page post receive? How many discussions are being generated daily in your group? How many people, on average, are engaging in said discussions?

  o Google+: How many +1s, comments, and shares does each post receive? How many discussions are being generated daily in your community? How many people, on average, are engaging in said discussions?

o YouTube: How many views, thumbs up, and comments did you receive per video? How many total YouTube video views did your brand receive?

o Pinterest: Take a sampling of your recent pins. On average, how many repins, likes, and comments are you receiving?

o Instagram: Similar to Pinterest, take a sampling of your recent images. On average, how many favorites and comments are you receiving?

- **Facebook tabs:** Because of Facebook's general strategic importance and the fact that you can have up to four visible tabs on the front page of a Facebook timeline, what are the four tabs displayed? In other words, what are your main calls to action for your Facebook fans?

- **Influence:** Although there is no one perfect algorithm to measure a brand's influence in social media, there are three platforms that allow us to publicly look up the influence of any social media user, whether person or company: Klout, PeerIndex, and Kred.[3] However, to easily monitor your competitors' numbers as well, the easiest platform to use for the purpose of this audit is Klout.

- **Social media presence on your home page:** When looking at your home page, where are your social icons? What social badges do you show? If I looked at a catalog of links to find out where to follow you in social media, how easily would I find them? Do you have a blog that is easily recognizable? Do you have a "social" page that aggregates all of your social content?

It's worth pointing out that, vis-à-vis a social media presence on your home page, there are two schools of thought to consider:

1. I don't want to show a social media presence on my home page because I don't want my precious website visitors to leave without converting them first.

2. I want my website visitors to know that we speak their language and are available for engagement on any platform where they are active. Furthermore, leaving our site to engage with us in social isn't necessarily a bad thing because if they begin to follow us without converting, at least we achieved a soft conversion, which keeps the opportunity open for a future conversion.

If your target demographic group isn't active on social media, this debate isn't important. However, if your audience is, the policy noted in the second point will be an important one for you to create. I personally prefer a phased approach: during those periods when I want to emphasize the social because we have campaigns or want to reach metric goals, I recommend placing social media icons and other widgets more prominently above the fold. However, if social reach is satisfactory, consider moving the icons to a bottom navigation bar or somewhere else where it is still discoverable but not as prominent.

Auditing your company's social presence is a good way to take note of what you are doing and determine what holes need to be filled. However, it takes on much more value when you compare your company to industry role models and create a spreadsheet comparing all of the above information.

INDUSTRY ROLE MODELS COMPETITIVE ANALYSIS

There is value in analyzing the social media activities of similar organizations in your industry to see what can be gleaned from a comparative analysis with the numbers generated from your social media audit. A look into the social media presence of these industry players whom you consider to be role models because of their market share lead, innovative marketing, or perhaps lead in social media activity will undoubtedly reveal some of the following points, which include generalizations based on my own social media consulting experience:

- Most companies at this time already have a social media presence. However, the social media channels used and the existence (or nonexistence) of a blog still varies widely, especially when considering the emerging social media channels of Google+, Pinterest, and Instagram.
- Social media reach, frequency, and engagement per platform vary widely.
- How competitors display their social media presence on their websites varies widely.

It takes time to compile these data, but having them available to analyze is well worth the investment. You will find that, in the case of most companies, a comprehensive and strategic approach to social media simply doesn't exist. This is indicated most glaringly by the lack of a blog or inability to find all social media channels in one place on a website. This nonstrategic approach sometimes results in large variations of tone between platforms. Likewise, it can mean your company is absent from the platforms your target demographic is using or your company simply isn't maximizing the use of each platform.

The details that emerge from such a strategic analysis raise a lot of questions regarding what your competitors' intent is in using social media. In the past, I've seen companies simply promote their own content without any engagement with followers, use social media as if they were issuing a press release, or even talk to their followers as if it were one-way communication. After completing this analysis exercise, you'll likely have a different view regarding who in your industry seems to be more effective in their social media program—as well as how current social media users and competitors probably view *your* brand!

The challenge with this analysis is finding meaningful and actionable metrics to use for your own social media strategy. For each platform, I recommend finding the competitor that seems to be doing best in terms of reach and engagement. How often does that company post? What type of content resonates best with its social media fan base? If you're lucky, you might find that your company leads your industry in a particular platform, but most companies will find plenty of role models to emulate for their own social media strategies. The metrics you create will become part of the comparative metrics I recommend you include in that section of your social media strategy, which we will discuss in Chapter 17. That said, I am a huge fan of standing on the shoulders of giants and leveraging the business intelligence that social big data provide all of us. If you don't use it for your company's benefit, your competitors might.

Now that you've audited your social media footprint and benchmarked your program with your competitors' publicly available data, you've undoubtedly started to generate lots of ideas about what to include in your social media strategy and how to optimize your preexisting social media program. It's now time to take these data and populate the heart of a social media strategy document.

Chapter 5   Core Elements and Concepts in Your Social Media Strategy

Based on my own social media strategy consulting experience, in order to create a comprehensive social media strategy, there are certain elements or concepts that must be in the actual document. Although there is general overlap among these concepts, they should be listed in the social media strategy individually to give the reader a better understanding of how they all work together. Note that the lengths of each of these sections will vary, with the channels section undoubtedly taking up the largest real estate.

BRANDING

The importance of extending branding guidelines to social media was discussed earlier in this book. Now branding guidelines must be brought in line with consideration to social media in the following areas:

- Naming
- Color scheme and imagery
- Voice

Naming

It goes without saying that every account in social media should be the same name as your company. However, there are three special circumstances to consider:

1. When the name you can insert into a username field is shorter than the name of your company, which is the case for many companies on Twitter. In this case, you need to prepare a shortened name for your company.
2. If you have extra real estate to use, utilize the name field of your social media account to add keywords to increase search engine optimization (SEO) and help others discover the account.
3. With an eye to the future, think about other naming schemes that may be necessary to localize the language or segment the purpose of the social media accounts.

At the beginning, the accounts should be singular in focus, representing the entire company. However, be cognizant of the name that you choose in terms of character limitation as well as potential SEO value.

Color Scheme and Imagery

Color scheme and imagery for a brand's social media presence should already be clearly spelled out in the brand guidelines and similarly adhered to in social media. Two areas, however, might be of particular interest in visual real estate and are probably not discussed in traditional brand guidelines:

- Cover photos that have extended real estate, which you can upload as part of the Facebook page and Google+ brand page
- Twitter and YouTube backgrounds

Both of these allow businesses to offer visual branding information and phone numbers, URLs, and other information to help guide users to other relevant information. This should be used if possible to help guide the public to other helpful resources above and beyond the content available on social media channels. Once again, traditional brand guidelines provide your company all the guidance needed in terms of visual imagery to use here, but you need to take advantage of that real estate to maximize its value.

Voice

The voice of a company in social media is equivalent to the tone of its conversations in tweets, Facebook posts, and blog posts. Traditional marketing communications often have a tone that might be deemed more appropriate for written communications, but in social media it is expected that a more conversational tone will be used. Because of the global nature of social media, and in accordance with your target demographic group, which might include the average consumer, make the effort to modify the tone so that it is more easily accepted by a broad range of social participants. This can be determined only after strategy implementation and analysis.

Third-party tools to help you analyze the readability of your content are available. One such way of testing the readability of your content is through the Flesch Reading Ease test.[1]

CONTENT

Executing the recommendations in any social media strategic plan will require sharing both unique and curated content in different frequencies in different ways on different platforms. Sharing relevant content helps cultivate brand awareness and thought leadership, and it fosters the communication of strategic initiatives to the public. Although it goes without saying that your own corporate news should be shared through your social media channels, an even better approach would be to also share content that you curate from other sources to become a channel that your targeted demographic group tunes into when engaging in social media to find information important to them.

Although social media is not about broadcasting and self-promoting, the followers of your brand might actually appreciate these types of messages, and thus they should be included with your social media content. However, when sharing such content, remember to keep self-promotion, especially of the automated kind, to a bare minimum and instead share content in which your customers might genuinely be interested. Sharing only relevant information in a meaningful and engaging way helps your company:

- Establish further credibility and positive goodwill.
- Become a brand that is truly in sync with the consumer and serve as a resource.
- Gain new website visits to build awareness for strategic initiatives from social media users who are reading and potentially sharing your content.
- Promote dialogue with social media users, which further helps with the previous three points as well as strengthens relationships and builds a stronger online community.

The types of content to share in various social media formats varies from company to company, but more than likely, the content strategy should be composed of a combination of the following types of content:

- New product, campaign, or service information
- New events or highlights from recent events
- Original blog post entries, which are ideally targeted articles based on a category/keyword strategy
- YouTube videos from your channel, customers, or events
- Photos of your latest products, customers, or events
- Conversations from other social media channels (cross-posting), such as responses to questions or surveys
- Engagement questions or quotes (especially for Facebook)
- Crowdsourcing content from your customers (guest blog posts, photos, videos)

o You could choose a guest blog post of the month to highlight when you have no original content to publish. This would be ideal if influencers or brand advocates agree to contribute their stories, tips, or ideas.

- Third-party information relevant to your customers or target users obtained via content curation or social media conversations (retweets, etc.)

Although sharing third-party information may seem counterintuitive, it contributes to building thought leadership in your industry and allows your company to contribute to conversations by serving as a resource for information. This content should be shared in a strategic combination with your own content, content from other industry thought leaders, content from influencers, and content generated by fans.

This is an important point because, unless you are a ubiquitous consumer brand such as McDonald's or Coca-Cola, it is sometimes necessary to share other people's information to spark the interest of those who might not yet be true fans. From an SEO perspective, this helps your company be found when users search terms relevant to the messages with which you want to engage the public. If you look at the keywords that bring most visitors to your website via search engines using your website analytics tool, chances are those keywords are associated with your company name or perhaps a place name that is part of your company name. If you are utilizing pay-per-click (PPC) advertising to target words that are not associated with your brand to attract relevant visitors to your website, these same words can be targeted as part of your content strategy for this social media plan.

Now that you know what type of content to share in social media from a holistic perspective, it's time to formalize the subject matter of the content that we are going to share by creating what I call content buckets. Content buckets are subject matter categories that help us rationalize content creation, curation, and sharing while creating a social media editorial calendar. Think about content buckets like this: If there are four subjects about which you want to attract social media users to follow you and visit your company's website, what would they be? I use the number four because I always recommend a minimum blogging frequency of once a week, which is equivalent to creating one blog post per category each month. This makes it much easier to manage the implementation of content publishing as part of the social media strategy.

Creating four content buckets is difficult for some companies. Here are some questions to answer to help you create your own:

- Can you organize your products and services into four distinct types?
- Can you divide the sales of your product, either actual or planned, into four distinct types?
- Can you organize the industries you sell to into four distinct industries?
- Can you segment your target demographic into four distinct types?

Completing this exercise will help you create your own buckets of content. The objective is to find silos of content to share that attract distinctly different social media users to engage with your brand; by doing so, you can see how the content you share becomes an important part of the social media experiment. If you can't narrow down your content buckets to four, that's fine. But the closer to four you can get, the easier it will be to manage. Conversely, if you have only two or three content buckets, look at ways of further dividing those topics to reach the magic number four.

These content buckets cover only content you will publish as part of your proactive engagement with social media users. Reactive engagement is covered in the engagement section later in this chapter.

CURATION

Content curation is an important part of implementing your social media strategy in that it provides relevant content to share—content that helps a business gain mindshare with social media users. It also lets companies be viewed less as marketing entities and more as community resources.

Content can be curated in many ways, and more than likely, relevant content will come from other news resources or even bloggers who are producing a large volume of content on the Internet. For some companies, simply curating photos uploaded by fans provides great content. Here are some ways to curate third-party website content to share on your own social media accounts:

- Look at what relevant content you and your staff read every day that your target demographic audience might find interesting.

- Do a search on Twitter search engines such as Topsy.com or Google "site:Twitter.com keyword" for relevant keywords and see what relevant news sources or blogs are being frequently retweeted.

- Create an RSS reader using a service such as Feedly,[2] NetVibes,[3] NewsBlur,[4] or The Old Reader.[5] This will allow you to curate content from blogs identified in the previous step. Once you do so, some of these services will automatically recommend other RSS feeds from similar blogs that might interest you.

- Continue to add, delete, and modify your RSS subscriptions so that your feed becomes a highly optimized and relevant resource, helping you keep your finger on the pulse of optimal content to curate and providing insight on topics your target demographic audience finds interesting.

Some may construe the publishing of third-party content as a promotion of that product or service. Confer with your legal team before curating and publishing third-party content.

CHANNELS

Social media has many communities, referred to as channels from a marketing perspective. Major social media channels where your business could potentially participate are noted in the list that follows. Selecting the right channels in which to participate has a great impact on the success or failure of the social media strategic plan. Use publicly available data found from conducting keyword searches, reading research reports, and utilizing self-service social ad platforms to ensure to the best of your abilities that the social media channel in which you decide to invest time is the most appropriate one for your business.

Although there is no golden rule as to how many social media channels in which you can or should participate (after all, each community is distinctly different), start by managing fewer social media channels and making them successful before moving on to conquer new ones.

- **Blogs:** Blogs will be the primary source of content for you to share in social media and thus help give your company a social voice. A blog is also appropriate for the inbound marketing[6] of your content to aid in brand awareness by making your website easier to find when consumers are searching online for information. Topics on which potential customers have an interest and would want to share with others are prime targets for blog content. Third-party blogs are also an important source of content from which to share—or repurpose and share—through your social media channels. In terms of blogging platforms, WordPress is the most popular content management system,[7] but Tumblr is also growing in popularity both as a blogging platform and as a social network with 170 million users.[8] It also has a distinct user base, of whom 50 percent are younger than 25 years old.[9]

- **Facebook:** A 1 billion+ user[10] community, this is the most populous global social media website, reaching one in every seven people in the world. It is the first or second most visited website in 33 countries as diverse as the United States, Pakistan, Argentina, Turkey, Indonesia, Mexico, and Brazil.[11] In the United States, more than 80 percent of time spent in social media is done on Facebook,[12] which now is where almost 11 percent of all online time is spent.[13] Facebook is quickly becoming the global white pages.

- **Twitter:** Twitter has been reported to have more than 500 million users[14] and was recently reported to be the fastest-growing social network in the world.[15] It is a site where the news breaks and information sharing spreads virally. It's also the default search engine for real-time search results as well as public search engine for conversations. Twitter has become a default social networking platform for television viewing, engaging with athletes and celebrities and watching live events.

- **LinkedIn:** LinkedIn is a community with 200+ million users.[16] This popular professional network is critical to every business-to-business (B2B) social media strategy while still having relevance to business-to-consumer (B2C) brands interested in engaging with business decision markers, pursuing a wealthy demographic group, and fostering B2B partnerships (alliance partners, distributors, etc.).

- **Google+:** Never publicly announced, Google+ is estimated to have more than 500 million users.[17] However, another report puts Google+'s active user base at 343 million, making it the second most active social network in the United States.[18] At the end of the day, Google+ is a self-proclaimed social layer[19] that ties together your relationship with all of Google's properties. It's no wonder, then, that active engagement on Google+ influences Google search results. Furthermore, the unique, growing community on Google+ makes it worthy of engagement similar to what is found on Twitter.

- **YouTube:** Similar to Facebook, YouTube also recently reached the important milestone of having 1 billion users.[20] It is the second largest search engine in the world.[21] Video is not only a preferred medium by many, but it's also the most powerful form of content in creating an emotional connection with the public.

- **Pinterest:** A nearly 50 million user community that is centered around pinning images to boards or collecting visual things of interest in categorized files, Pinterest is unique because it hit 10 million monthly unique visitors faster than any other website.[22] It is estimated that 83 percent of its global users are women,[23] and it drives more average sales per user from referring visitors to other sites than any other social network.[24] Pinterest is now the fourth largest referral of web traffic worldwide after Google, direct input, and Facebook.[25]

- **Instagram:** This community of 100 million users[26] lets people share photos from their mobile devices. It is the largest mobile social network and is owned by Facebook, so if visual content is an important part of your content strategy, the Instagram user base cannot be ignored.

- **Forums:** Forums and chat rooms can be considered the beginning of social media as we know it. However, the trend today is that these forums have either migrated to popular social media sites or social networking sites have been created around the forums themselves; thus, they are not included in many social media strategies. If you think there might be a relevant community in a forum somewhere, start by doing keyword searches on Big Boards,[27] the best forum search engine that I know of; it displays the number of members and posts for each forum. You might also find specialized forums on Ning.com.

- **Others:** Many other social media channels exist that might be more relevant than those just listed depending on your social media strategy. I've done my best to list those mentioned in most of my social media strategy consulting sessions, but you should also consider adding the following channels if they seem appropriate for your company:

- o Digg (social news site with 10 million users[28])
- o Reddit (social news site with 43 million users[29])
- o StumbleUpon (social bookmarking site with 25 million users[30])
- o SlideShare (presentation and content sharing site with 45 million users and recently acquired by LinkedIn[31])
- o Foursquare (geo-locational check-in mobile social network for restaurants, retail, hospitality, and brick-and-mortar stores in urban areas with 25 million users[32])
- o Yelp (review site with 78 million users[33]; especially important for restaurants, retail, and brick-and-mortar stores)
- o Flickr (photo-sharing site with 87 million users[34]; popularity has been on the wane for some time, although its owner Yahoo! recently redesigned the site and is enticing users to come back by offering them 1 terabyte of free photo storage[35])
- o uStream (site for live event streaming with 60 million monthly users[36])
- o Podcasting (Although 25 percent of Americans reportedly listen to podcasts,[37] the fact that there are only 250,000 podcasts registered in iTunes,[38] compared with 14.5 billion pages indexed on the Internet,[39] means that it might be easier for your relevant audience to find you via podcasting if your target demographic is an avid consumer of them.)
- o Wikipedia (as a contributor)

FREQUENCY

Personal users of social networking sites don't need to think about how often they use the sites and can do so in a natural and organic way. Companies are obviously different: resources are limited, but the number of activities you could be engaging in on social media is limitless. This is why, as part of your social media strategy, it's important to set guidelines as to the frequency in which you will be proactively publishing content to each platform.

Although you can probably never publish too much to a particular platform, it's important to note that social media users are getting bombarded with more and more content on various platforms,[40] so you should always adhere to a frequency strategy as long as every single piece of content you publish is of high quality and represents your brand. Furthermore, if content is king, consistency is queen, so once you start, it's important to create a consistent dialogue with social media users.

I recommend three different types of frequency strategies based on the type of content or channel you are posting to for the major social media channels. For newer channels or those described in the "Others" section in the preceding list, take an approach similar to my recommendations for Facebook and LinkedIn and begin slowly:

Blogs and YouTube (Unique Content That Is Indexed in Search Engines)

Blogging and uploading videos to YouTube are the best ways to create your social voice to be shared throughout social media while reaping SEO benefits. To make an impact from an SEO perspective, the more frequently you blog, the more content gets indexed by Google and thus the more opportunities you have to appear in search results. Likewise, the more blog posts you have, the higher the chance that someone in your target audience will click the content and share it in social media, giving you even greater reach. However, creating content will be one of the most, if not the most, resource-intensive exercises you undertake; this is especially true of creating videos. With that in mind, my recommendation is, at a minimum, to aim for blogging weekly and posting to YouTube monthly. As you begin to catalog your digital assets and repurpose evergreen content for blogging, you should slowly increase this frequency to two or even three times a week as long as you are confident that you have a healthy inventory of blog posts to publish from in the future. Once you have been able to gauge the return on investment (ROI) of your unique content creation, consider increasing this frequency as part of your regular social media review.

Being able to submit your blog to Google News is the ultimate in SEO and would result in significantly more exposure because your blog post would be displayed in the "News for" section, which often appears at the top of the search results. However, it is said that, in order to be approved by Google, you need to have a history of 40 to 50 blog posts each month. Furthermore, it is necessary to have multiple authors to represent your blog. Although seemingly unrealistic for many businesses to consider right now, it is a lofty goal that you should set for the future once blogging becomes a natural activity for your organization, especially if you can recruit bloggers throughout your organization or get guest bloggers from your community of users to regularly contribute.

Facebook and LinkedIn (Relatively Infrequent Posting Platforms)

Facebook is a tricky platform in that businesses are tempted to frequently post new content to engage with their audiences, but Facebook prevents most messages from reaching most fans because of its use of EdgeRank to filter out what users see in their News Feed. Furthermore, there is no other social network where businesses are operating on the private territory that many of us keep that has defined Facebook until now. Therefore, it is no surprise that in order to optimize posting for EdgeRank and ensure that every posting is of a relevant and high quality to their audience, most page owners stick to posting 2 to 3 times a day.[41] My recommendation is to start posting conservatively once or twice a week, work your way up to a recommended once-a-day posting schedule, and then slowly increase to two or three posts a day once you are confident you can maintain the frequency and you see increased engagement.

LinkedIn is a completely different platform than Facebook, but it is similar in that many people still consider it a personal, albeit professional, platform. Users thus were never accustomed to the frequency of updates that have plagued platforms such as Twitter, making them seem "noisy" to many. I once liked a few status updates in my network feed, and one of my connections complained that I was being too active because every single update showed up on his network updates feed.[42] With this in mind, the posting frequency for Facebook can be equally applied to LinkedIn; it is a network where you want to value the quality of your posting over the quantity.

Twitter and Google+ (Noisier Platforms)

Twitter's nature requires frequent posts to be found and heard above the noise. Therefore, compared with other social media channels, it is acceptable to post more often here. A good goal of posting new content, should there be a sufficient number of updates available to post, is to do it at least as frequently as you do on Facebook and LinkedIn. Should you find yourself easily curating content, post at twice the frequency of Facebook and LinkedIn. This may mean beginning by posting two to three times a day and then increasing to a potential four to six times a day.

As mentioned before, Google+ is similar to Twitter in that there is a need to post somewhat frequently to be heard above the noise. Furthermore, because it is Google, there are inherent benefits to posting more frequently. Therefore, the same recommendations for Twitter hold true for Google+.

It bears repeating that a frequency strategy as recommended here is only a guideline. There is no one right or wrong frequency strategy. Ultimately, it depends on how much quality content you have to share and how much each of your unique communities is engaging with you.

ENGAGEMENT

Engagement in social media for the purpose of your social media strategy is divided into two parts:

1. **Proactive** posting of both new content and conversations, as well as the sharing of content and information from others
2. **Reactive** conversations with social media users responding to those who reach out to your social media profiles through commenting or messaging

LISTENING

It goes without saying that it is vital for every company to listen to what its customers who are active in social media are saying about the company or even saying to you without directly speaking to your brand. It is important to note a distinction between a narrow reactive engagement strategy where you are simply responding to social messages and comments directed at you and a broader listening strategy to glean insight from conversations that are not directed at your company.

Every day there are conversations occurring in social media that cannot be tracked because many users do not properly tag companies when they converse on social media. In fact, according to one study, only 3 percent of tweets directed at a company actually use their official @username.[43] In these conversations, your target audience may be discussing your company or services. Conversations about what people are saying about your industry, competition, and company can be analyzed for further information. Furthermore, to track the ROI of this strategy, some of the metrics (such as comparative metrics to competitors) can be more effectively measured with the help of social media monitoring tools.

Most companies and brands monitor social media conversations with third-party software that either archives or searches conversations from Twitter, Facebook, LinkedIn, YouTube, blogs, forums, and other social media channels in real time. Each platform differs on content coverage, number of allowable search keywords, sentiment analysis, reporting capabilities, and historical cache, among other things.

Social media monitoring is normally recommended as part of a phased approach in consideration of the education and resources necessary to implement the strategy. In an ideal world you would listen before you engage. In reality, though, social media monitoring software is an expensive investment and should be used only once you have created your social media voice and presence on the platforms.

CAMPAIGN

Social media campaigns are essential to continuously engage with fans, attract new ones, and experiment with finding content, types of content, and channels that resonate with social media users. For this reason, social media campaigns using a variety of content topics, types of content, and channels are recommended to increase fan engagement, grow the user base, and experiment with each community.

Social media campaigns should not be confused with traditional campaigns that are used in marketing to promote new products or discounts. Social media campaigns should leverage the social aspect of social media combined with the viral functionality to create events that trigger engagement from followers in a new and exciting way.

There are many different types of social media campaigns, but some easy-to-understand examples of campaign types are:

- Surveys, quizzes, and polls
- Crowdsourcing photos, videos, and content
- Product giveaways

Campaigns should be implemented on a monthly basis around revolving themes, such as those aligned with promotional, calendar, or seasonal events. They should be used to break up content monotony and begin new conversations with present fans and general social media users.

INFLUENCERS

If you already know who your influencers are, you simply need to find where they are on social media and on which platforms they are most active. If you don't know where to start, begin by defining those social media users whom you think would be considered influencers. They are usually part of the target demographic group consisting of individual users, companies, or media outlets that are a part of or serve your target demographic audience and yield influence online. They do this primarily through reporting/blogging but also by being active in social media on platforms such as Twitter, Google+, Facebook, and LinkedIn.

There is no one standard for determining influence in social media. That said, the following types of websites provide data that can be used to measure influence:

- Social influence: Klout, PeerIndex, Kred
- Blog authority: Technorati, PostRank
- Social numbers: Facebook fans, Twitter followers, Twitter lists, LinkedIn Group members, LinkedIn company followers, Google+ circlers, RSS subscribers
- Website rankings: Alexa, Compete
- Social engagement: number of retweets/Facebook shares, etc.
- Frequency of engagement: frequency of blogging, tweeting, Facebook posting, etc.

Notice that these metrics are similar to the statistics that we compiled as part of the social media audit.

At the minimum, influencers provide a source for content curation, and by retweeting their content, it raises the chances that they will notice you and reciprocate the favor, thus broadening your reach in social media.

Beyond merely utilizing influencers for content curation and to broaden social media reach, they should also be considered as potential collaborators in future social media campaigns.

BRAND AMBASSADORS

Brand ambassadors are critical for helping spread the word about your brand through their social networks and acting as an advisory board to tap into during a crisis as well as when business needs arise. For the purpose of a social media strategy, consider a brand ambassador as someone who is a loyal fan and also very active in social media. Ideally, brand ambassadors will be selected similarly to how potential influencers are selected, but with one important difference: these individuals are already customers and fans of your brand and thus can be trusted—and should be rewarded—at a fundamentally different level.

A brand ambassador program helps fans spread the word and value of your brand throughout social media. Customized programs, similar to the types of campaigns that were listed in the influencer outreach section, should be created with the needs of both the fans and your company considered to create a true win-win relationship.

CRISIS MANAGEMENT

Crisis management and social media communications will be covered in depth in Chapter 14, but note that not every brand requires a thorough crisis management section in the social media strategy. However, if you already have a crisis communications strategy, it is a best practice to include how you plan to integrate social media with it. This is an important first step. Given the speed at which information travels in social media and how social media is now a primary place for consumers and the media to turn to for updates on the latest information, many think it is inevitable that some sort of "crisis" will occur.

Although traditional crisis management strategies look at crises that resulted from company assets, employees, or customers, with the advent of social media, there is always the possibility of an attempted takeover of social media channels by fanatics and others with an agenda. These scenarios should also be included in any crisis management preparation.

A first step in using social media for crisis management is to become more proficient at using the social media tools themselves. The strategic plan should outline specific steps to help company employees become expert users of all channels deemed strategic and implement best practices recommended as part of the social media strategy should a crisis strike.

A second step in the crisis management strategy is to proactively build a community of goodwill with social media users and followers of your brand. Over time your word will become more trusted, and more brand advocates will be born. This will definitely help lessen the potential negative effects of any crisis. This is why responding to all questions and conversations in social media is critical in establishing and developing this positive rapport.

Although this is a fairly comprehensive list of possible elements to include in your social media strategy, you might need to include others down the road. Regardless, those elements noted in this chapter should provide enough guidance that you have the confidence to create a robust and comprehensive social media strategy.

Chapter 6   Blogging as an Essential Part of Every Social Media Strategy

Blogging is often misconceived in the business world as being something for personal discussions only, but statistics show that 28 percent of Fortune 500 corporations already have blogs,[1] and it's becoming as much of a communication medium for businesses as it is a personal one. I talked about determining your social media objectives in Chapter 3, and one of the common objectives businesses have in creating a social media program is generating website traffic. Although platforms such as Facebook, Twitter, and LinkedIn may succeed in driving traffic to your website, there is a slight disadvantage in that content on these sites isn't owned by you; that is, it's content that is residing somewhere other than your website. Using a blog becomes a rational strategy in creating content that can be shared and amplified through social media channels and that will ideally bring people back to your website.

HOME BASE

If your business is going to be active in social media, what will it say and how are you going to draw people to your website, where they can make a purchase, learn more about your products, or act on some other objective they may have? Social media channels such as Twitter don't provide a lot of space to convey what your company does, so your blog becomes your home base—the central hub and part of your website that establishes your authority or voice. By creating content on your blog, you're able to convey your company's point of view and then share that content through social media. Because you share from your home base, you bring people to your "home" from your various social networks.

SOCIAL VOICE

How will you talk about the things you want to discuss in social media? You must communicate with people on their terms. As mentioned earlier, social media is made for people, not for businesses, so sharing blog content provides the opportunity for businesses to interact with fans on a human level. A blog is a perfect way to communicate in a more social voice, rather than the strict business voice you might be using for your regular website content. Blogging also serves as good practice for developing your social voice and learning the best ways to communicate with your fans online. Sharing your perspectives as a person, versus as a company, through the blog allows people to have a longer, more in-depth conversation with you. It's clear that by using a blog to establish your social voice, your overall voice on social networks will be enhanced and you'll be able to more efficiently create amplifiable content.

SEARCH ENGINE OPTIMIZATION (SEO) AND INBOUND MARKETING

Statistics show that people spend as much time online now as they do watching television.[2] Of the time being spent online, the most popular actions are searching for information, using e-mail and chat applications to communicate with others (which is why it's also important for businesses to continue with their e-mail marketing), and spending time on social media.[3] A blog is unique in that not only does it help maximize your social, it also helps maximize your SEO.

If you have an e-commerce site, you have hundreds, if not thousands, of pages on your website that you manage. But a lot of companies, especially small businesses, have only 10, 20, or 30 total website pages. By adding a blog, you're adding an additional host of content to your site. Say you have 20 pages of content on your site—about, contact us, products and services, and so on—that results in 20 or so pages. Each is indexed individually by Google. If you start blogging once a week, which is the minimum frequency I'd recommend, you add 52 pages of new content to your site over the course of a year. This triples the number of pages on your website from 20 to 72 and therefore triples the amount of content now indexed by Google; in essence, that triples the chances that, for any combination of keywords out there related to your business, your content will show up in the search results.

A blog has tremendous potential in helping your company maximize its social and also be found by search engines. Some people like to refer to blogging as free search engine marketing. Obviously, how well written and relevant your content is and how many social signals[4] you're receiving from your social content, along with Google+ and Google PageRank, affects how discoverable your posts become. Statistics show that companies with blogs receive 55 percent more website visitors, 97 percent more inbound links (inbound links are links on the Internet to your website, which helps determine your Google PageRank score and the influence of your content), and 434 percent more indexed pages than companies that don't have blogs.[5] This is strong evidence supporting the notion that blogging helps your SEO and inbound marketing in addition to the other advantages noted here.

WORDPRESS

Hopefully by now I've reconfirmed the importance of having a blog for your social media strategy and inbound marketing. Another important component to consider is the infrastructure of your blog. There are many content management systems (CMSs) out there, but I always recommend WordPress as the best CMS for a blog based on experience. If your current enterprise website already has blogging functionality, there is no need to change. However, if you're on a site that doesn't have this functionality or would like to start a brand-new blog, consider looking at the ease of use and free open source technology that WordPress provides.

Many agree that WordPress is the best CMS. A recent study showed that of the top million websites on the web, WordPress had a 63.71 percent market share.[6] In many cases, it may not be best to work with the guerilla in the market; however, in this case, WordPress is highly recommended. It's stable and has an extensible architecture with plug-ins, meaning that whenever a new social media site emerges, you can easily download a plug-in to incorporate it into your site and leverage that social network. In fact, WordPress as a CMS can also become an entire website for small businesses. Many small businesses I've worked with that hadn't updated their sites in years made a simple transition to a new WordPress site. My website, MaximizeSocialBusiness.com, is a great example of a site run completely on WordPress, including the blog.

Another important thing to note is that there are two different versions of WordPress: WordPress.org and WordPress.com. WordPress .org is recommended because you can take advantage of the extensive architecture and plug-ins that it provides, including plug-ins that are not available on WordPress.com. Some of these plug-ins, for instance, allow for the automatic creation and distribution of your own XML site map to search engines that index the content. Other plug-ins allow you to easily optimize meta titles, meta descriptions, and keywords for optimal SEO.

CONTENT BUCKETS

In the previous chapter, I discussed content being one of the core elements in a social media strategy. I also described in detail how a content strategy should include content buckets, which means dividing the content you want to talk about into four different buckets (or topics). This makes it easy to manage blogging activity and optimize it based on the PDCA framework in order to get a feeling for what kind of content resonates best for different audiences. This allows you to optimize your blog and social sharing for even greater results with your blog. As mentioned, I recommend blogging at least once a week. If you're following this model, creating four content buckets will provide content for an entire month by focusing on one topic each week, making a blog easy to manage.

Let's take a look at a concrete example of content bucket creation. One of my social media consulting clients owns a brick-and-mortar garden store. The business received 50 percent of its sales from traditional flowers and trees and the remaining 50 percent from things like landscaping work for homes and businesses, as well as events or weddings. This breaks down into four different areas of content: flowers, trees, landscaping, and events. Look at your current sales and see if you can divide it into four different categories. Better yet, assess where you want your sales to be 12 months from now and see if you can create four different buckets based on that. If you can find only two topics, see if you can create subcategories. If you have more, try to narrow them down to four main categories.

If blogging gives you an SEO and inbound marketing advantage, you also want to consider keywords for your blog posts. You likely always had an SEO strategy for your website, whether it includes keyword campaigns, pay-per-click (PPC) advertising, work with an SEO company, or even a review of your web analytics to see what keywords are driving people to your website.

Other tools are available as well, my favorite of which is Google Suggest. You'll notice it when you go to type something into Google and it automatically brings up the 10 most common search phrases that are used with the terms that you're entering. One thing I like to do is type "LinkedIn" to see what kinds of things people are searching about regarding LinkedIn, and then I'll write blog posts about those topics. If you're trying to think of topics to write about, incorporate a keyword strategy like using Google Suggest into your content plan.

It's important to keep in mind that you shouldn't blog about what *you* want your customers to know but rather what *they* want to know. The one-way broadcasting approach in social media doesn't work. You want to try to get into the head of your target demographic group as part of your social media strategy and really determine what kind of content interests them. Or, think about it this way: What do they need to know that they don't know they need to know? Given the answer to this question, create shareable content to leverage the amplification potential of social media. Because this content sits on your own website, it will attract people to your website and indirectly market your company and showcase your credibility. The best advice I can offer regarding blogging is to create content that is shareable and resourceful.

Your social media content strategy should align heavily with your blog strategy. Publishing a blog post once a week provides you with something to consistently talk about in social media, gives people a reason to visit your website, and, as you become comfortable with this blogging frequency and learn what kind of content does well by reviewing Google Analytics data, allows you to see the return on investment of your blogging efforts.

Chapter 7   Maximizing Your Facebook Presence

If you look at all the social networks side by side, Facebook is the largest, with more than 1 billion users. It's also the most playful and the place where everybody is hanging out. It's kind of like the white pages; if you ever wanted to advertise to people, that's where they'd be. And it's not just an American phenomenon: the site features more than 20 million users in several countries globally. As noted earlier, 50 percent of the user base is older than 35 years of age, so Facebook is not just for younger people. It embraces people of all the demographic characteristics.

This huge potential of Facebook challenges every single company to leverage it for the viral aspect and capture friends of fans when your fans share your message to their network. A look at who our average friends are gives you an idea of the influence our fans can have.

A study by the Pew Research Center reports that the average number of friends a Facebook user has is 229. Some of us may have a lot less, and some may have a lot more. A point of interest from this report is that our Facebook friends are generally former high school or college class-mates or family members,[1] which is not necessarily the case on LinkedIn or any other social media platform. Therefore, the friends of our fans are some of the most trusted people in their network, and to whom do people turn when they want recommendations or feedback? They go to trusted friends or family. With that in mind, friends of Facebook fans are considered the Holy Grail to many marketers, and this is what makes Facebook such an enticing platform.

If you represent a business-to-business (B2B) brand, you may not have thought to use Facebook as a social tool; however, the number of people using Facebook for business rather than personal use is on the rise. I read two studies that focused on doctors and dentists that noted that these groups tend to use Facebook more professionally than they do other platforms such as LinkedIn or Twitter. With that in mind, and because businesses do business with other businesses, they're actually conducting it with other people in those businesses. Because there are definitely ways to engage in a B2B perspective on Facebook, companies should consider having a Facebook page as part of their strategy.

One of my clients is a company that provides chemicals to environ-mental consultants, and the company has been successful using Facebook to engage their clients. The company has turned its Facebook presence into a very engaging environment because those same environmental consultants who spend time on LinkedIn during the weekdays are also spending time on Facebook on weeknights. These professionals enjoy learning about their work, viewing videos and photos of industry-related products, and otherwise engaging with various other things related to their profession.

EDGERANK

EdgeRank is to Facebook what the Google search algorithm is to Google. Google has a secret algorithm that decides what content gets to the top of the rankings for each keyword, and the average company spends a lot of money trying to get its content to the first page of Google search results. With the advent of Search, plus Your World, which I'll discuss in Chapter 10, search results are going to be even more personalized. In comparison, your Facebook News Feed, which is where studies show people spend the most time,[2] is also using an algorithm to determine what content shows up there. Similar to Google, it is a secret algorithm that is constantly changing so that it can't be exploited by users, but we do have some information that Facebook has offered regarding what this is. EdgeRank helps determine which of your content is seen and therefore most likely to cause engagement by as many people as possible, so it is critical to learn about this to maximize your Facebook presence.

Facebook has divided factors determining EdgeRank into three parts: affinity, weight, and time decay.

Affinity is your relationship to the creator of the content. Let's put it this way: it's common knowledge that we are closer to our friends than brand pages; therefore, the relationship with friends might mean that content from them will have a better EdgeRank than content coming from brand pages. Because of this, some small-business owners I know have actually stopped posting on their page and have turned their personal profile into a quasi business page by leveraging the EdgeRank their personal profiles have. This may not work for everyone, but it's an example of how important the affinity is for EdgeRank.

Affinity also deals with how often you engaged with content from a particular person. If there's someone whose content you've liked, commented on, or shared, that means you have greater affinity with that friend and therefore you're going to see that person's content more often in your News Feed. There's a tactic called engagement that we'll talk about in the next section that will help create a greater affinity with your fans so that they'll be able to see and subsequently engage with more of your posts.

Another factor is *weight*, which is the type of content posted: photo, video, link, or status update. Although there are other types of content such as that from third-party sites, events, and so on, these form the four primary categories of content that most utilize. Data have shown that photos and videos are the most engaging content,[3] although this can vary for each Facebook page depending on its fans and the content they engage with.

Facebook is a business, and its main revenue generator is ads. Therefore, the more engaging content that shows up in the News Feed and the more you interact with it, the more time you'll spend on Facebook. And the more time you spend on Facebook, the greater the chances are that you'll be clicking on those ads and promoted posts within Facebook. This explains why photos and videos seem to be getting more prominence in your News Feed than other types of content. Because photos typically do so much better than other types of content, if you want to post a link to your site, consider sharing a photo and including a link back to your site within the photo description rather than posting only a link. The photo has a greater chance of appearing in the News Feed of more fans, and thus it has a greater chance of engagement.

The life span of a Facebook post is referred to as *time decay* and is, unfortunately, not very long. Unless there's a lot of engagement with it, the average life span of a post is estimated to be as little as 3 hours.[4] Most people usually comment, like, or share posts within the first couple of hours of publication, and this is when it is more likely to reach more fans. Timing of your post is critical; therefore, tools that analyze the best times to post become even more important. Keep in mind that most companies are actively working Monday through Friday 8:00 to 5:00 but most people are active on weeknights and weekends, so experiment with using tools, such as EdgeRank Checker,[5] that will help you find the best time to post.

EdgeRank is critical to understand and optimize because otherwise, your message won't be heard by most fans; even Facebook officially acknowledged that, on average, only 16 percent of your fans will see any given content that you post.[6]

ENGAGEMENT

Engagement should not be one of the objectives for your social media strategy. It is a specific tactic in Facebook to increase your EdgeRank because the greater number of likes, comments, and shares received on posts means you'll have a greater affinity with a greater number of fans and a better chance of showing up in their News Feeds.

If you look at posts that big brands and others publish, there's a formula for those that seem to generate the most engagement. Your target audience, branding, and strategy determine what you share and how you share it, but it is worth noting which posts seem to drive the most engagement:

- **Questions:** Asking questions generates engagement because people feel the need to answer. Similar to ending blog posts with a call to action, asking questions works well in social media, especially in Facebook. Make sure the questions you ask are relevant to your community.
- **Fill-in-the-blanks:** Fill-in-the-blank posts also get a lot of engagement. "I like Mondays because _____." It is easy for fans to throw in their thoughts. Obviously, the more relevant, witty, and creative it is for your community, the more likely you are to have people fill in the blank.
- **Calls to action:** The easy call to action is also efficient. "Like this post if you're looking forward to the weekend!" Like asking for a comment at the end of a blog post, using a call to action is an easy way to get people to interact with your content. Obviously, you don't want to go overboard. I've seen pages where every post starts with "Please like this post if . . ." This can easily turn people off from your content.
- **Feedback requests:** Crowdsourcing ideas is great. Ask for an opinion about your product. Consumers feel empowered when they have a voice, and giving your customers a voice is a powerful way to narrow the gap between your brand and your fans, in addition to garnering engagement on Facebook.
- **Posts with visuals:** Expressive visuals can be combined with questions, commentary, and campaigns.

Interestingly enough, there's a tool called Post Planner[7] that helps build engagement. Take a look at it if you need ideas or feel stuck with engagement on Facebook.

FACEBOOK ADS

Many social media marketers believe that social media is free; therefore, why would anyone pay Facebook (or any other social network) to post an ad or move your post to the top of your fans' News Feeds? My response to that is social media has never been free. It's an investment in time and resources. In a social media budget, perhaps a small amount of money is for tools or software, but most expenses are going to be related to people—employees, consultants, and agencies. With that in mind, maximizing paid social media beginning with Facebook ads can be a great way to accelerate meeting your goals.

There are three main types of ads that you are most likely to use: page ads, page post ads, and promoted posts. Page and page post ads attract people to like your page or get them to like or engage with a particular post by using ads placed on the right-hand side of a user's Facebook page. It should be noted that the right-hand side of a Facebook screen is visible only on the website version of Facebook. From a mobile perspective, the preferred approach to get your posts to show up in the News Feed is to promote one of your posts, which is the ultimate way to defeat EdgeRank and ensure your posts get maximum visibility. Promoting your post means paying money to ensure more of your fans see your post in their News Feed. Put simply, promoting posts generates more engagement and ensures your post is seen by more of your fans.

Page ads are used to acquire more Facebook page likes. This can be extremely effective when you're just launching a new page; maybe you have a new goal of reaching 500 or 1,000 likes within 10 days, and you have only a few left to go. Sponsoring your page can be an inexpensive and quick way to meet your business objectives. You can also use page sponsoring to make sure you meet monthly or quarterly goals and supplement organic growth your Facebook page has achieved.

Page post ads are unique in that you're driving people to a specific post. This might be used if you have a campaign on Facebook or a specific post advertising an upcoming event. Instead of having to go to your Facebook page to see the link to the specific promotional thing, Facebook users can potentially click directly from the ad. Think of this as providing assistance so that people don't have to take extra steps to reach something specific you're promoting on Facebook or your website.

As far as pricing goes, the average cost per click (CPC) in the United States has recently been cited between $0.26 and $0.33.[8] These numbers are lower than average compared with advertising with Google AdWords, which costs more than $0.50 per click globally.[9] I've implemented Facebook CPC ad campaigns that ended up being much cheaper, but pricing varies according to a number of variables. Facebook ads give your business the ability to generate tremendous brand awareness in a targeted community for as little as $50 or $100. Some people have had concerns about Facebook stock prices going down, but I think the future for Facebook ads is a bright one, especially as the company looks into ways of improving mobile advertising revenue.

Another thing that makes Facebook ads extremely valuable to your business is the ability to microtarget them. You can't do this with a promoted post, but you can with a page ad or page post ad campaign. Using specific criteria, you can direct your advertising to a number of different regions or categories: age, gender, location, and precise interest. In addition to selecting from broad categories, you can target people who like certain Facebook pages. For instance, people who like a competitor's page or similar page or those who have specific buying habits can be targeted. You can target people who are fans of your page or those who are friends of those who like your page. There's a lot of power here that is not available anywhere else in the online ad world.

As with any social media usage, there are best practices for Facebook ads. Facebook wants to publish ads that are going to be relevant to people who will likely click on them and not see them as having a negative impact on their user experience. Therefore, Facebook has a stake in your ad's success, as it is a win-win-win if they generate ad revenues, the user is happy with the decision to click, and you are happy with the outcome. The greater engagement your ads get, then, on average the cheaper they become over time. To increase the odds of a higher click-through rate (CTR), provide multiple ad options for publication. Think of creating an ad as having a matrix of nine different combinations. On top, there are three different columns, each representing a different age and gender: for example, males 18 to 25, males 26 to 30, and females 31 to 45. These categories would come from the target demographic data assessed earlier. You can customize image and text completely so that you can create three different sets of text and images for each demographic group. This results in nine different ads that will be distributed to the proper audiences. Facebook will then look at which ad was most successful in terms of CTR and show it more often, driving down the CPC over time. This is a very specific way to use Facebook ads to reach a target demographic group in a cost-efficient way, and the advice comes straight from the source: Facebook's own Ads Optimization Guide.[10]

To use page post ads, target those who like one of your competitors' pages. Create five different ads for people who like five different pages. Facebook will find the one that does the best, which will be displayed more and probably end up costing less.

It's important to note that promoted post cost at the present seems to be cheaper than page post ads because it's going out to fans who already know you and should therefore be engaging more with your posts than strangers would anyway.

Understanding which type of ad to use in different situations is important if you want to leverage advertisement as part of maximizing your Facebook presence. For those curious, there are a number of case studies publicly available that reveal the positive return on investment (ROI) from advertising on Facebook: the dog kennel that spent $30 in ads to sell a $1,350 puppy to fans for a 4,400 percent ROI[11]; Samsung spending $10 million on Facebook ads to promote the Galaxy S3 during the iPhone 5 launch and generating $129 million in sales solely from Facebook[12]; and All Nippon Airways (ANA) using target keywords such as *anime*, *sushi*, and *sakura* for things associated with Japan, hoping users would like going to Japan with the airline and ultimately achieving a 25 percent CTR and positive ROI from conversions.[13]

FACEBOOK CAMPAIGNS

Facebook campaigns are important because no other social platform allows you to embed other applications or content from third-party sites into your company page and do something creative with it. As noted, social media is a never-ending experiment, and a campaign is a great way to experiment with fans to see what intrigues them and gets them to act. It also allows you to keep things interesting for fans. For my social media clients, I like to create editorial calendars so that every month they're doing some sort of campaign.

Facebook campaigns can be used specifically for a number of different tactical objectives. Many things can be done with a Facebook application embedded inside a tab on a Facebook page. Some of those things are:

- Increase fans by "like gating" the Facebook campaign, which means that only those who like the page can enter. Those who enter can also share with friends and recruit others to become new fans as well.
- Increase engagement with current fans and entice their participation and engagement.

- Build an e-mail list. Most companies aren't able to carry Facebook fans over to a mailing list. You can set up a campaign to accept e-mail addresses as a requirement for entry.
- Drive traffic to a Facebook page or website.
- Encourage specific product or service sales.
- Gather customer survey data. Use a questionnaire to acquire data to more efficiently implement and optimize a Facebook strategy.
- Crowdsource ideas and build community, thereby creating brand awareness and educating the customer.

Before launching a campaign, be sure to review Facebook's campaign rules, listed here.[14] Many people break them, but it's important to know what the rules are before proceeding with a campaign, such as:

- You can run a campaign only through a third-party application. A third-party app is one developed by a company other than Facebook (including yourself) that gets added to your Facebook page as a tab.
- You can't use liking or commenting on a post or uploading a photo to the page as means to entry. This is because Facebook doesn't want you to dupe EdgeRank; instead, they want all of the activity for your campaign, with the exception of promoting it, to take place in a tab removed from your main timeline.
- You must notify winners outside of Facebook, which seems ironic to many. This can be done via a blog post, Google+ post, tweet, or direct e-mail. After that, you can link to the announcement on Facebook.

Once you understand the rules, you need to look at the many applications available for Facebook campaigns. There are many out there with prepackaged options that you should consider, and a short list of platforms worth considering include Wildfire, Binkd, Involver, Easypromos, Woobox, Pagemodo, Shortstack, Heyo (formerly Lujure), North Social, and Tabsite. (If you do a search for Facebook campaign or promotion apps, you'll find a number of other companies that do this, but these are the ones I'd recommend investigating when determining what company's platform to use.)

Because each of these app platforms offers prepackaged options, all you have to do is customize and then launch your campaign. Take a look at what each offers in terms of campaign options—contests, coupons, sweepstakes, photo submissions, and so on—to get an idea of what's possible with Facebook campaigns. I highly recommend using campaigns as part of your experiment with Facebook.

FACEBOOK INSIGHTS

Facebook provides a Google Analytics–type application for your Facebook page. If you're the administrator, you can access this by going to the page you manage when you are logged in and clicking on the See All link to the right of the Insights link. This tool provides a great amount of data that allows for further maximization of Facebook.

Insights has four different screens: Overview, Likes, Reach, and Talking about This.

Overview is where you learn about the actual performance of each of your posts. This is critical to understand what's working and what's not in terms of time and day of the week posted, types of posts, and actual content of the posts. It provides information on reach, which is basically how many News Feeds your content has reached. When discussing EdgeRank, I find in many cases that only 5 to 10 percent of fans see your content. Divide your reach by the total number of fans to get the approximate EdgeRank for each of your posts. See which posts had greater and less reach, and ask yourselves "Why?" Those answers hold the keys to understanding the mystery algorithm that is EdgeRank.

Talking about This refers to fans who generated activity on your Facebook page, which thereafter created a story in their News Feed. These could be people who liked, commented, or shared your post or who responded to an event; basically, anyone who engaged with your content. This is the critical metric you're looking at for engagement. In general, the more people talking about this, the higher the overall reach for your content. Facebook thinks the Talking about This number is so important that it displays the number publicly on each page next to their number of likes.

Then there are engaged users. Engaged users are people talking about this, in addition to generating a click on something. Facebook defines this as the number of unique people who have clicked on your post. People who have engaged or clicked on a post are considered engaged users, and those who took the extra step to like, comment, or share would also fall under the talking about this umbrella.

At the far right is a column for virality, which sounds like it's an important metric but in reality it's basically the Talking about This number divided by the Reach number. It indicates, of the number of people who saw your post in their News Feeds, how many people are actually engaging with it. Some posts will be high in reach, others may be high in engagement, and still others may be more viral. It's hard to analyze all these different things. The best overall assessment is to look at the posts that had the highest or lowest of all of these factors when trying to understand what happened and why, and then replicate that formula to optimize your Facebook posting.

The Likes tab provides information on the organic or paid likes the page received over a period of time. Incidentally, it also shows the unlikes, which can be critical if you are posting too frequently or promoting too many posts that perhaps clog up the News Feeds of your fans, prompting them to unlike your page. Looking at the unlikes can be just as important as noting the likes. This is also where demographic data, including everything from gender and age to countries, cities, and languages of your fans, are stored. Another important thing to note is where the like sources came from. Did people like the page from their timeline, a Facebook recommendation of your page, third-party apps, a Like Box from your website, or your fan page? Understanding the source of your likes can be worthwhile.

The Reach tab looks at those we've reached either organically, through paid options, or via the viral spread of content to friends of fans when a post was published. As compared with likes, this provides interesting information, such as unique users by frequency; if you're doing a lot of paid advertising to get people to visit your page, what's going to be the difference between the organic, paid, and viral reach? Are there any differences in reach demographics versus like demographics that may unearth telling information? Is there interesting information regarding tab views? Finally, where are people coming from when they enter your page from outside of Facebook? Are they coming from your website, Twitter, YouTube, or somewhere else?

The Talking about This tab provides demographic and location data for those who are generating activity according to this metric; it also provides a chart to show the viral reach from that activity. These demographic data provide critical information, especially when compared with reach and likes.

Spend time poking around Facebook Insights if you haven't already. It is a treasure trove of data that should be used as part of a data-driven social media strategy to optimize your Facebook presence.

Concentrating on these five critical areas, you can truly maximize your Facebook presence so that your activity on this social media channel will always be optimized and as effective as possible to achieve your social media strategy.

Chapter 8   Maximizing Your Twitter Presence

Twitter is often one of the least understood social platforms for businesses, but it can be valuable regardless of whether you're in a business-to-business (B2B) or business-to-consumer (B2C) industry. I believe it's an essential tool to help maximize your social media presence.

After Facebook, Twitter is the second most popular platform used by businesses.[1] Eighty-six percent of marketers have reported using Twitter as part of their social media marketing efforts.[2] In addition, the percentage of Fortune Global 100 companies with Twitter accounts has been reported to be higher than the number of companies with Facebook pages, YouTube channels, or corporate blogs.[3] Those that do use Twitter are likely to have several different accounts to segment their messages—from a general marketing account to separate ones for each product to a dedicated customer support account.

If you still don't believe in the importance of Twitter, here's some food for thought: more than one-third of marketers who are using Twitter said that it was critical or important to their business.[4] That flies directly in the face of the misconception that Twitter is all about what people are eating for breakfast. Quite simply, it is an essential part of social media marketing and a critical business platform to have a presence on.

PUBLIC NATURE

Twitter and Facebook may have a few similarities, but there is one huge difference. Facebook is full of, in essence, private profiles and conversations. If people are using their privacy settings properly, very little of what they talk about is open to the general public. Their updates are broadcast only to their friends. In fact, with the way that EdgeRank works, very little of that content goes out to their friends anyway.

Twitter, on the other hand, is an extremely public platform. When you create a profile you have the choice to create either a completely public or completely closed presence. Just by doing a search on Twitter, you'll find that 90+ percent of the profiles are public. That means every tweet can be searched—and not just by people following your account. Anyone can search, find, and use a tweet for any business intelligence or other purpose. If this seems irrelevant, consider a study conducted that showed there were as many searches on Twitter as there were on Google and Bing combined.[5] That makes Twitter the second or third largest search engine in the world after Google and YouTube. In addition, the content on this search engine is in real time, so it's by far the biggest real-time search engine in the world. No other social media platform currently has the real-time reach that Twitter does. Later we'll talk about Google+, which is emerging as a competitor to Twitter, but for now, Twitter is the best way to grow your influence and publish in real time.

Companies have public relations (PR) departments and invest in media relations to get the word out about their company. And if that is important to you, Twitter deserves your attention, because the platform really is, at a minimum, free PR for your company.

If you're still not convinced, here is a test I do with every single one of my skeptical clients that you should do, too. Go to https://twitter .com/search-advanced to access the advanced Twitter search page. Enter some keywords that are relevant to your company, brand, competitors, or target audience. Regardless of what niche industry you're in or how unique you think you are, you'll probably be able to find people talking about your products or products like them, your industry, or even your company itself. It works for everyone!

One of my clients trains auto dealership salespeople. The president called me in because he wanted help on LinkedIn. I suggested that we take a look at Twitter, which he didn't think had any value. We did this simple test, and lo and behold, posted was a picture of a salesperson sleeping at one of his dealership trainings. He wasn't happy about the photo, but needless to say he was surprised that his business was even receiving Twitter exposure.

Another one of my clients specializes in providing information related to energy trading prices—stuff like where the newest pipelines are being built and where there are new natural gas finds. It's a very niche industry, as you can imagine. When we did a search on Twitter, we found that one of his competitors had already accumulated a robust Twitter following and had an engaging Twitter presence.

SOCIAL MEDIA DASHBOARDS

Taking part in the conversation on Twitter can be complex because of the limited functionality of the Twitter website. Twitter.com has a very simple interface, and although it's gotten a little richer, it's still not as complex as Facebook, Google+, or LinkedIn. There's not a whole lot there except your updates, a list of notifications concerning those who have interacted with you, and the unfiltered updates of everyone you're following. It can be incredibly overwhelming.

One advantage Twitter does have is its application programming interfaces (APIs). APIs allow third-party developers to create apps to increase the functionality of Twitter, and there are hundreds, if not thousands, of these apps out there. You will find that most people who tweet don't actually do it on Twitter.com. Unlike other social platforms, Twitter users are tapping into the site through third-party apps. There was actually a survey I did that showed that the most tweets being created by social media influencers were done on HootSuite, a social media dashboard. Twitter.com came in second, with another Twitter app, TweetDeck (which Twitter also bought), coming close behind in third.[6]

Given Twitter's limited functionality, there's been an ecosystem created around it to help individuals and companies get more out of their tweeting, which is why these apps have been created. Most of these apps fall into the category of social media dashboards, like HootSuite. Although these tools were initially created for Twitter, they have expanded to include other platforms as well. To maximize your Twitter presence, you definitely want to find the right social media dashboard for you and loop in as many other social platforms as you can to create a one-stop space to help efficiently manage your social presence. There are several options, but here are a few of the best:

- TweetDeck (Since Twitter bought out this platform, you can expect it to become more tightly integrated with Twitter in the future.)
- HootSuite
- Sprout Social
- MarketMeSuite

For the small-business market, these are the leading platforms for which you can accomplish a great deal of social media management for less than $99 per month. Other platforms with richer feature sets and deeper analytics—and higher price tags—are available, but it is recommended you start small until you see the return on investment from your efforts.

Choosing the most appropriate social media dashboard for your company is one easy way to assist you in maximizing your Twitter presence in a variety of ways. Following are the features you should be analyzing when comparing dashboards:

- **Multiple accounts:** Most companies have multiple Twitter accounts, and if you're using Twitter.com, you can access only one at a time. When you're using a dashboard, you can post from any of your accounts at any time. You can post the same message to several accounts at once or only one.
- **Integration with Facebook and LinkedIn:** Twitter.com doesn't offer integration with other social platforms, but these dashboards do. TweetDeck can also help manage postings to Facebook, but HootSuite goes further by connecting users with Facebook, LinkedIn, and Google+ pages. Sprout Social and MarketMeSuite can also be used to post to LinkedIn and Facebook, as well as Foursquare and a

few other social channels. These integrations help save time on your overall social media marketing efforts.

- **Tweet scheduling:** The key to a consistent Twitter presence is to keep your stream going, but that's difficult if you're using Twitter.com, where you have to keep logging in to post updates throughout the day. With a social media dashboard, you can schedule tweets so that they show up at prearranged times. Many dashboards provide users with bookmarklets, which are added to your browser's toolbar, allowing you to add updates from wherever you're surfing online.

- **Autotweeting:** HootSuite, Sprout Social, and MarketMeSuite allow you to autotweet from an RSS feed. This ensures your new blog posts are automatically added to your Twitter account when they go live.

- **Archiving tweets:** When you start working on Twitter marketing and growing activity on the platform, you'll start to get more @username responses and interactions per day. In many ways, it becomes a bit like a social media inbox. On Twitter.com, you're not easily able to decipher the tweets to which you've responded, and this can become confusing as you become more active. With Sprout Social and MarketMeSuite, you can archive a tweet after you've taken action. This doesn't delete the tweet, but it hides it from your view to keep your dashboard from appearing cluttered. It's a functionality that truly helps you maximizes your Twitter presence.

CONTENT CURATION

We've already discussed a frequency strategy with other social platforms; for example, you'll want to publish a blog post at least once per week, and with Facebook, try posting once or twice per day. Be careful, however: post too often on Facebook, and you might be perceived by some as even spamming them.

With Twitter, things are a bit different. It is such a noisy platform that frequent tweeting doesn't necessarily stick out as appearing to be spam. If you're tweeting only once or twice per day, you're going to get lost. You need to stay more active on Twitter than you would with other platforms (except for maybe Google+, but we'll get to that later).

With this increased frequency, the problem then becomes how to fill those publication spots in your social media editorial calendar. On platforms that require significantly less publication, it's easier to find content for an audience, but you can't post five or six tweets per day on the same weekly blog post. That's where content curation comes in.

In discussing the social media strategy process, we made note of the types of content about which to blog and share. Great content you create should be centered on what your current customers and prospects want to hear. The same is true for curation, which requires sharing other people's content that will keep your brand's mindshare with your potential audience. No matter what industry you're in, by tweeting relevant and interesting content from your industry, you'll attain the same mindshare as if it was coming from your own company.

In fact, you can build a deeper trust, because with content curation, you're not just promoting your own business. Curation is all about selecting the very best content for your target audience from authoritative third-party sources—just like you'd curate art for a special exhibit in a museum. This doesn't mean you have to share content from your competitor, but every industry has reliable, interesting content that is available to share beyond a few single sources.

By doing searches on Twitter, which was covered earlier in this chapter, it's easy to find a lot of relevant content that you can simply retweet, but you should also seek out content to curate from original sources. Where do you find this content? Think about what you read each morning and what is important to you as a member of your industry. Whether you're subscribed to industry newsletters or getting blog updates through an RSS feed, there are probably several sources that you're already using. These can be great sources for curation.

If you aren't keeping your finger on the pulse of your industry yet, now is the time to start! Feedly[7] and other RSS readers will help you keep track of the latest news so that you can review content and share it. When you come across something interesting, either tweet it right away or set it up for later publication. If a particular site is a really good resource for your industry, you can even have the RSS feed directly imported into a social media dashboard, which we discussed earlier in this chapter. This way, you'll automatically tweet everything from that source as it becomes published.

You can also retweet messages from accounts with which you want to align your brand. To keep track of the people with whom you want to rub virtual elbows, you'll need to create lists either on Twitter itself or through your social media dashboard.

To find the right Twitter profiles to add to lists, look for companies or people who are posting a lot of great authoritative content and would be a good resource for your target audience. When you retweet their content, you align your brand with them and increase the chances that they may follow you and retweet your content as well.

Although there is a need to post frequently on Twitter, it is possible to tweet too much self-promotional content. Many people have proposed specific ratios for how much curated content you should post compared with your own content. My personal rule is very simple: never tweet self-promotional content unless you feel like you absolutely must. If you can stick to that golden rule, you're going to build a lot of goodwill and trust with your audience. In fact, the click-through rate on any self-promotional tweets that you do end up posting will likely be a lot higher than if you simply publish self-promotional tweets.

Another guideline for mixing your self-promotional and third-party content is the 4-1-1 rule, which was first published in 2009[8] and popularized thereafter by the founder of content marketing as we know it today, Joe Pulizzi.[9] As an example of tweeting six times a day, the formula would look like this:

- *Four* tweets with original content (curated from authoritative sources)
- *One* retweet of someone else's relevant content
- *One* self-serving tweet, for example, your own blog post or campaign

Follow this ratio, and you'll be in good company.

Through content creation, you can increase your publication frequency, become aligned with important influencers, and most important, become a valuable source of information for your target audience. It's an essential strategy for Twitter, and the same concept can help you maximize your social presence on other platforms as well.

TWITTER CHATS

Twitter chats give you the ability to engage and potentially have your content amplified by a large number of Twitter users, many of whom have a large number of followers.

Twitter chats are unique to Twitter alone. There isn't really anything else like it on another platform. Because Twitter has a very public nature, people can interact with a large group by following the same Twitter hashtag at a prearranged date and time. They can join in a conversation just as they would have in an America Online chat room back in the early days of the Internet.

To understand how Twitter chats work, you need to understand hashtags. Essentially, hashtags are a way to categorize tweets and make it easier for other people to find content on the same subject. You can search for other people having a conversation on a similar topic by searching for a hashtag, for example, #socialmedia or #football. There's a way to optimize your tweets for search engine optimization using hashtags, but for the purpose of this section, we're going to focus on the social nature of Twitter chats.

Twitter chats are happening all the time, and if you want to join one, there's a great Google Drive resource that is regularly updated with a complete list of more than 100 of different Twitter chats on a variety of topics.[10] To understand how it works, search for a Twitter chat that is relevant to your industry. Once you've found one, listen in on it first. You can easily follow the conversation by adding a search column in your social media dashboard with the hashtag for the chat.

Once you understand how things work, you can jump in and start participating. I recommend using a Twitter app such as TweetGrid to help you be efficient in participating in a Twitter chat.[11] Getting involved in a Twitter chat is a great way to help your brand make a splash in the social media community, assuming that you're sharing relevant content and adhering to the etiquette rules.

Dun & Bradstreet is an example of a brand that has successfully leveraged Twitter chats for exposure and engagement.[12] Even though it hasn't sponsored a Twitter chat of its own, the company has been able to grow its Twitter accounts through chat participation. The company's retweets and mentions increased by 50 percent thanks to their chat contributions, and the company has had multiple invitations to guest host chats.

I recently interviewed Shelly Lucas,[13] the senior marketing manager at Dun & Bradstreet, and she had the following advice for brands that want to leverage Twitter chats for themselves:

1. Review the chat questions before the event. These are often posted on a blog or Facebook page. Think about them. Spend 5 or 10 minutes jotting down ideas for answers. Check your bookmarks/RSS feeds/social posts for relevant material.

2. Before the chat, retweet the host's tweet announcing the chat topic and guest host and frame the post or craft a tweet of your own using the chat's hashtag. This gives your own followers a heads up that your Twitter stream will be very active for the duration of the chat; it also invites your community to join.

3. Some chats move very fast, so using TweetChat, Twitterfall, or similar tools can be very useful. I use TweetChat, which allows users to control the refresh speed and "smart" pause the chat. It also automatically adds the chat hashtag to your tweets.

4. Introduce yourself at the beginning of the chat. This is especially important if you're a first-time participant or relatively new to the chat or if you're tweeting as a brand.

5. Engage by adding a comment when you retweet someone else's contribution. This can be as simple as "+10," "Bingo!" "Well said!" or "True–esp. when . . ." If you don't agree, by all means, retweet or respond accordingly and/or ask for clarification, but always respect the opinions of others.

6. Avoid spamming chat participants with shameless product or service promotions unless someone specifically asks for more information. Tweeting a link to one of your own blog posts is usually accepted within moderation, as long as it's relevant to the conversation.

7. Ask questions if relevant. Often, a related question will pop into my head while I'm chatting. If it's relevant to the topic and within the scope of participants' expertise, I'll tweet it with the preface: "Question for everyone . . ."

8. That said, avoid sidetracking the chat with extended one-on-one or niche group discussions. Exchanging a few tweets is fine, but if it goes on too long, it can exclude others and distract from the chat host's agenda. Wait until the chat is over to pick up the conversation.

9. At the end of the chat, tweet an original and sincere thank-you to the host, guest host, and anyone who made the chat more worthwhile to you. Be sure to follow those folks whose contributions you found especially valuable.

Although Dun & Bradstreet has relied on Twitter chats arranged by others, there's no reason why you can't create your own chat if you feel there's a need in your industry. Here's how to run a successful Twitter chat:

- **Stick to a regular schedule**. Whether it's weekly, biweekly, or monthly, you need to be consistent with a Twitter chat so that people know what to expect and when to show up.
- **Promote your chat**. Create promotional tweets for your chat so your followers (and hopefully their followers) will participate.
- **Create compelling content**. The topic of your Twitter chat will be the biggest selling point. Find some hot-button issues or problems people want to solve. These can stimulate conversations. You can also interview thought leaders or employees at your company. As long as you make it interesting, people will engage!

There's no better way to get in front of a lot of people than to participate in a Twitter chat, but you need to pay attention to these etiquette rules in order for them to be advantageous. Once you think you've maximized your Twitter followers to the extent that you can on your own, joining or running a Twitter chat is like the final frontier of maximizing your Twitter presence. Keep looking and experimenting with chats until you find the right one for your brand.

ADS

In the Facebook chapter, we discussed ads on that platform and how social media is never free. Don't feel ashamed about advertising or feel like it's against the rules of social media. The same is true with Twitter. By investing in advertising on Twitter, you can significantly accelerate your social media activities.

Twitter has a self-serve platform similar to that of Facebook and has been busy enhancing it after a relatively late introduction. Compared with Facebook, your advertising options are simple: you can promote your Twitter account, or you can promote your tweets. When you promote your account, your profile shows up in the "Who to follow" section on the Twitter home page. When you advertise your profile with Twitter, you can increase your follower account more quickly than you could on your own.

You have a few options for targeting Twitter ads, and the menu of options recently increased (although they aren't as many compared with Facebook). For promoted accounts, you can target location, interest categories, gender, or @usernames, which targets advertisements to people with the same interests as followers of specific users. Promoted tweets allow you to additionally specify where you want your ad to appear (search results, timelines, or your own profile), in addition to having the option of targeting specific devices and platforms when targeting search results or timelines. When you target your Twitter ads, Twitter will help you find the right users within its available parameters, but they aren't as specific as with Facebook advertising.

Doing a promoted Twitter profile ad campaign can help you achieve certain goals or get a new account off to a good start. Promoting specific tweets, on the other hand, is an option if you want your followers to take a specific action. The goal with promoted tweets is often to entice people to click through on a tweet and visit the linked page. This is similar to page post ads on Facebook.

There have been a number of case studies on the success of promoted tweets. One is from Optify, a digital marketing software company. The company's promoted tweet campaign created a 770 percent increase in leads and a 600 percent increase in referral traffic from Twitter, and conversion from Twitter traffic increased 6 percent.[14]

Pricing for Twitter ads can vary, but I did an experiment to see how much it would cost to grow my follower list (in a reluctant manner) by 1,000 over 30 days, and the total cost was $332.19. A second experiment with different parameters over the same time period yielded a similar $0.365 per new follower. You can buy fake followers, but there's no reason to do so when you can advertise to real people on Twitter who are relevant to your brand. In addition, these people have opted in to follow you; they have interest in you, they are active on Twitter, and they thus are more likely to engage with your brand in the long term.

As far as promoted tweets go, I've found that it's very similar to my Facebook cost-per-click (CPC) experience. I've had Twitter-promoted tweet campaign CPC pricing go as low as $0.13 per click. The pricing is always in flux for ads of both types, and if you're able to narrow your focus and get really targeted, your price could be even lower than what I found during my experiments.

Experimenting with Twitter ads is a smart move if you want to maximize your Twitter presence, and with the changes Twitter has made to its ad platform, you now have actionable analytics to use to learn more about your Twitter followers, your activity, and your ad performance—available only for those with an ad account. For that reason alone, it's a smart idea to open a Twitter ad account.

The very public nature of Twitter makes it unique and often overwhelming. However, taking the time to learn how to use the tools available to communicate, create, curate, manage, and promote your content in this medium makes it much easier to maximize your Twitter presence as an essential part of your social media strategy.

Chapter 9   Maximizing Your LinkedIn Presence

Looking at the general spectrum of social media sites, with Facebook being on the far end as a large, personal site, LinkedIn is far on the opposite end of the spectrum as a professionally geared site with only a quarter of the number of users that Facebook has. However, LinkedIn is more about the quality of users than the quantity. Although this chapter will cover why LinkedIn is an important platform for business-to-business (B2B) companies, it's just as important for business-to-consumer (B2C) companies because every B2C company has both B2B components, such as partners, distributors, and strategic alliances, as well as a huge numbers of employees or former employees who can become brand ambassadors as well. Those who are your brand ambassadors on LinkedIn are a relatively influential demographic, and companies who want to be taken seriously should capitalize on and leverage LinkedIn as part of a social media strategy.

B2B

LinkedIn from a demographic perspective is very different from other social media channels in that it has a very influential, affluent, and educated audience. According to reported data, more business decision makers, people with household incomes exceeding $100,000, and college and postgraduates are LinkedIn users than the physical distribution audience of the *Wall Street Journal* or the *New York Times*.[1] This scale of influence that LinkedIn users have when compared with these leading business sites should not be underestimated, and because the household income stats are so robust, if your company wants to reach wealthy consumers as part of a B2C social media strategy, using LinkedIn may be a better choice than other options such as Facebook.

Because business decision makers are on LinkedIn and because B2B business involves selling to decision makers within companies, LinkedIn is obviously the best social platform to be active on. Statistics show that for any business, LinkedIn has been the channel where companies have acquired more customers than from a company blog, Facebook, or Twitter.[2] A similar study shows that, for lead generation and more specifically visitor-to-lead conversion rate, the conversion rate on LinkedIn is almost three times higher than that for both Facebook and Twitter.[3] It makes sense because LinkedIn focuses more on quality than on quantity. LinkedIn obviously doesn't have the high schoolers or preteens who are pretending they're high schoolers on Facebook, and it doesn't have the immense noise found on Twitter. For B2B, LinkedIn should be the preferred channel for your social media strategy.

PROFILE SEARCH ENGINE OPTIMIZATION (SEO)

With so many business decision makers on LinkedIn, you'll want to make sure that the profiles of your key outward-facing employees in sales and marketing are found should someone be searching for them. A popular activity on LinkedIn is looking at the profiles of other users, and there were more than 5.7 billion professionally oriented searches done on the platform in 2012.[4] Furthermore, your LinkedIn profile allows you and your employees to become brand advocates by sharing your company's updates in your status updates. Although LinkedIn is a personal network, in this way it provides companies a unique way to leverage the personal profiles of each employee and build an army of brand advocates sharing your message to their networks.

When I say profile SEO, don't limit that meaning to only your own personal profile. Have your employees, and especially the outward-facing ones, create a robust, SEO-optimized profile that is going to help them—and, indirectly, your company—be found on more profile searches. This all begins with the realization that your LinkedIn profile is your home page on LinkedIn. Your company likely spent a lot of time investing in strategies for your home page, and if your company and employees could all spend a bit of time strategizing how to optimize their LinkedIn profiles, especially for the outward-facing employees such as sales and marketing team members, it will be a huge benefit to the company.

With this notion of profile SEO, companies should create an SEO-optimized paragraph or paragraphs that employees can put in either their summary or employment background. Obviously, you should consult with an employment lawyer before asking employees to do anything related to social media channels, but if you make it voluntary and present it as a way for them to be found by customers, this is actually a great benefit to both the employee and employer.

The LinkedIn search engine, like all search engines, runs on a proprietary algorithm, but use the keywords and locations for which you want to be found and check the order in which your employees show up. Look at the profiles of the top three results for clues on how those individuals have optimized their profiles. Use this as a template to optimize your own so that you show up higher in those ratings. The LinkedIn search engine does update in real time, and although it can bring up different results for different people, if you follow these rules you should slowly find yourself appearing in more search results.

That said, you'll occasionally find profiles that are overly stuffed with keywords to the point where, when you click on the profile and notice this, their personal brand and company brand are actually going to suffer. You don't want to be a keyword stuffer, but optimizing keywords does matter, so work on finding middle ground. In my last book,

Maximizing LinkedIn for Sales and Social Media Marketing,[5] one of the case studies was of an accounting consulting firm where the president used the term *consolidation* in his profile; when the client who accounted for 50 percent of his sales in 2010 contacted him, the client said he was the only person in Belgium in the accounting industry who had the term in his profile and that's how they found him. The value of ensuring that all relevant keywords are included in your LinkedIn profile cannot be overemphasized.

GROUPS

LinkedIn Groups are the biggest forums for professionals on the Internet, and when you think about it that way, their existence is a boon to companies that want to join communities looking for customers and clients or those looking to create their own communities.

At last count, LinkedIn had more than 1.5 million subject-specific groups,[6] with the largest having more than 1.2 million members.[7] Groups have targeted discussions that allow users to virtually network worldwide 24/7. It's also important to note that if you're in the same group as someone else, even if you're not directly connected to them, you have the ability to send them a message as a result of being in the same group, which can help scale sales and marketing efforts. You can join 50 groups, and I recommend joining 50. You can join big groups just by doing a search on LinkedIn Groups with no keyword entered. The results are usually displayed in descending order by number of Group members, so you're able to quickly see which are the biggest groups. Local groups are also effective if you search for where your headquarters are located or, preferably, where your ideal customer is located. Alumni groups for your universities, employee groups for past companies, target market groups, industry groups . . . there's no lack of groups you can join, and by joining several, you can take part in focused discussions and message a greater number of other users. It is worth noting that you must represent a person and not a brand or company to join a LinkedIn Group.

How does joining LinkedIn Groups allow you to attract new business and customers? This is my personal case study of joining a LinkedIn Group, subscribing to a few weekly digests, reading those discussions that seemed to be heated, and waiting for an opportunity to jump in.

Someone in a group mentioned they were looking for social media expertise, and when I looked at his profile, I noticed serendipitously he was located locally. I reached out and asked to meet for a cup of coffee, and it turns out he was looking for social media expertise for a client he had. One week later, I closed the deal, and shortly after, that same person introduced me to another deal. Whether it's through tweets, Google+ conversations, or LinkedIn Group discussions, there are a lot of seemingly random conversations happening in social media. Behind a conversation, there might just be an undivulged business problem that people or companies have, and once you start engaging, they may reach out to you or you can reach out to them and find those business opportunities.

Another case study from my last book involved a gentleman named James Filbird,[8] who basically does what I did on LinkedIn Groups every day to a grand scale. He spends time engaging, meeting people, and taking conversations offline; according to his account, being active on LinkedIn contributed to 75 percent of his $5 million business. The more time he spends on LinkedIn Groups, the more business he's able to create.

There's also business value in creating your own group and developing a community within LinkedIn. If you represent a large brand, it could be a good idea to start an alumni group of current and former employees. Another case study from my last book was regarding a woman named Lanette Hanson[9] in North Carolina who runs a small business that hosts an annual event called the California Worker's Compensation and Risk Conference, which she also created a LinkedIn Group for.[10] The group had only a little more than 1,000 members at the time, but they drove 60 percent of her business for that year.

LinkedIn Groups aren't just for small businesses to attract new business; they are also for larger brands to become thought leaders in their industries. Phillips is a brand known as a role model for companies on LinkedIn. Phillips created its own health care–focused group called Innovations in Health, which I also highlighted as a case study in my previous book. It has more than 70,000 members[11] and is one of the top groups in the health care space. Preliminary market research on their target demographic of doctors and hospital staff revealed that they both spent a lot of time on the Internet and appreciate the opportunity to be a part of communities that allow for the sharing of ideas and information. After finding out that more than 5 million medical professionals were already on LinkedIn, they put one and one together and created their own LinkedIn Group. The group has generated thousands of discussions, and 60 percent of group members are at manager levels and above.[12]

Other larger brands have been successful in creating their own groups and engaging with LinkedIn users. Chevron has one of the leading groups for professionals in the energy industry,[13] while the Hewlett-Packard Personal Systems Group in the United Kingdom created a group to offer advice to small and medium-sized businesses that has helped them gain influence within this target demographic.[14] Creating your own community within the lucrative community of business decision makers on LinkedIn is one way to truly maximize your LinkedIn presence.

COMPANY PAGES

Company pages give LinkedIn users the ability to follow your company just as they can on Twitter or like your page on Facebook. Although many companies neglect their LinkedIn page, some companies, such as Hewlett-Packard, actually have more than 1 million followers for their LinkedIn company page,[15] which demonstrates the potential of attracting a large number of followers within LinkedIn. Users can follow LinkedIn company pages, and representatives for the brand can also post status updates, which go to the feeds of the company's followers. LinkedIn company pages also have their own search engines, so there are benefits to filling out your profile completely. Companies can also add services, and once some are added to the page, users can recommend those services, which adds an element of immediate social proof. Someone visiting a company page might recognize others within their network who might have already endorsed a particular product or service.

Status updates sent from your company page can be optimized. Facebook has a similar feature of being able to optimize and target where to send a status update, and LinkedIn actually offers additional ways of using those microtargeting options. You can customize everything from company size and industry to corporate function, seniority, and geography to ensure that only relevant messages reach relevant users.

Once you build your company page, just like establishing a new presence anywhere else in social media, you need to promote your page in order to attract followers and kick-start organic growth. Another case study from my previous book is the brand Rypple, which has since been acquired by Salesforce.com. Rypple first had their employees introduce their new company page to their network. Once you follow a company on LinkedIn, that action is revealed to your connections on your LinkedIn network updates. Shortly after building up a page following from this promotion, they started noticing that 70 percent of new page followers came from outside their employees' networks. The net result from all of this was that the company ended up seeing a 25 percent increase in traffic to its website from LinkedIn, along with a 10 percent increase in new user sign-ups from LinkedIn. Establishing a company page is the easy part: promoting it and engaging with your followers through relevant status updates on a consistent basis can help your company establish greater influence in the LinkedIn community—and generate new business—requires a strategic approach.

LINKEDIN ADS

LinkedIn ads are exciting because, similar to Facebook, you can precisely define and target who sees your ads. They can be targeted by geography, company name, industry, group, gender, and age. The ability to target in this way is compelling: if you want to target only chief executive officers (CEOs) of 20 different companies, you have the ability to do that. People in groups are probably most active on LinkedIn, so targeting them can be very lucrative. Ads can also promote your company page or even have others recommend products and services that you've already built into your company page.

The important thing to realize about using LinkedIn ads versus Facebook ads is that it's about the quality user demographic over quantity, so if you're trying to sell a 99-cent product, LinkedIn may not be the best use of your advertising budget. It should be noted that, from my experience, LinkedIn ads tend to be priced higher than ads on other social media platforms, so consider the quality of the type of company you're targeting. Like Facebook, you should create numerous ad variations to determine the one that has the higher click-through rate (CTR) so you get more impressions and therefore have a cheaper cost per click. From my experience, compared with Twitter and Facebook, CTRs tend to be lower on LinkedIn.

One case study of a LinkedIn ads success story is Volkswagen India, which wanted to raise brand awareness in a market where it was relatively new.[16] The company used LinkedIn ads to send people to its company page, and within 30 days, it gained 2,300 new followers and 2,700 product recommendations. As a result, it achieved more than 960,000 viral updates about Volkswagen car models within the network updates of LinkedIn users.

LinkedIn ads are often a forgotten component of LinkedIn, but it bears repeating that if you have not experimented with them yet, it can be a very cost-effective way of helping meet your company's social media strategy objectives.

LinkedIn is a complex platform that offers various functionalities because you can leverage the personal as well as the corporate by having outward-facing employees both represent the company and themselves in their LinkedIn interactions and communications. Because of this, LinkedIn offers tremendous potential for both B2B and B2C brands to leverage the potential brand advocacy of their employees in addition to their sponsored groups and company page.

Chapter 10   Maximizing Your Google+ Presence

Most people reading this book probably aren't surprised that I had a dedicated chapter to blogging, Facebook, Twitter, and LinkedIn. But a chapter dedicated to Google+? Maximizing your social is all about optimizing your presence on all the social media platforms, and at this point, Google+ has already become a major social networking platform that once again transcends both business-to-consumer (B2C) and business-to-business (B2B) industries.

Google is integrating Google+ with many other products, which brings many people into the Google+ fold. As a result, as I mentioned in Chapter 5, recent statistics indicated that Google+ was the second most active social network in the United States. This is proof that Google+ deserves your attention, and after reading this chapter and the special report on how Google+ is changing the online world, hopefully you'll better understand why having a presence on Google+ should be an integral part of your social media strategy.

SEARCH, PLUS YOUR WORLD

Google made its most significant change to its algorithm when it introduced Search, plus Your World in 2012.[1] If you're not familiar with this, it basically provides personalized search results for Google+ members when they do a Google search. For example, if those you have circled (similar to liking a person on Facebook or following someone on Twitter) have +1'ed a page or post of yours (or liked, in Facebook terms), their actions are now influencing the search results you see. Google has always said it wanted to provide the most personalized, effective, and relevant search results possible, so it only makes sense that, through Google+, if we tell Google the people, brands, and media outlets we like to follow, we'll see search results based on those preference filters. People who have Google+ see that they're getting personalized results; not only does this affect the way we see search results, but we also see Google+ posts appearing in search results now. Usually I see one or two Google+ posts per a page of 10 results. If you do a search for a company or a person, you may actually see his or her Google+ page in the results that allows you to like that person (or company) right then and there from the search results.

At any given time, people on the Internet are likely active in social media, conducting web searches, or communicating through e-mail, which is why you need to have a social, search engine optimization (SEO), and e-mail marketing strategy. Google+ can single-handedly affect your SEO just as significantly as your blog, if not more so. One example I recently saw: when I type "thank you" into the Google search engine, the first result is thankyou .com, but the second result is from someone in my Google+ circles named Judy Gombita, who is one of the bloggers at Maximize Social Business on the topic of public relations and social media. This second item in the search results led to a post that merely began with "Thank you [so-and-so] for sharing this article . . ." It's things like this that are showing up in the search results that relay the absolute strategic importance from an SEO perspective of why every business should have at least a minimal presence on Google+.

Another example pertains to a Japanese rental conference room company where I knew the name of the company but not the website URL. I did a search for "nano space meeting room" in Japanese, and the main result—above the company's own website—was a very simple Google+ post that the company wrote. Obviously, Google+ is about much more than the SEO, but hopefully you begin to see the impact that Search, plus Your World and Google+ are having on the search world. It should be no surprise, then, that one study found that those companies with a strong Google+ presence showed a 42.6 percent increase in website traffic compared with those without one.[2]

SEO

Just being active on Google+ will absolutely affect your SEO. To be most effective, you obviously want to be found and have others to circle and engage with you. By having a Google+ profile, you basically have a PageRank,[3] which is similar to what a website does. Our Maximize Social Business Google+ contributor Mark Traphagen will reveal more details about this in his fact-finding special section that concludes this chapter.

From an SEO perspective, it's really about sharing things to attract others to a page and build authority like companies do with a website. We can also compare content shared on Google+ to that shared on Twitter, which is used to broadcast information beyond our own companies and attract more people to follow us as we become a more resourceful channel for them. With Google+ posts being indexed sometimes faster than blogs, if you don't have time to start a blog, you could even consider using Google+ to microblog in order to attract the SEO benefits. Having a Google+ profile is not enough, though; you must create a robust, engaging platform. Hopefully, some of the advice here, as well as in the Twitter chapter, will assist with that.

With every follower on Google+ who +1's one of the blog posts that you share from your website, your chance of that Google+ post appearing in the search results of your follower's followers grows. In fact, in the final proofreading of this book, new data suggested that receiving Google+1's was more important from an SEO perspective than even the number of backlinks.[4]

CIRCLES

The more circles or people that follow you, the more influence your posts have as those followers of people who have circled you may be influenced by your circles sharing or +1'ing your content. This is comparative to why friends of Facebook fans are important. Facebook does not allow pages to friend fans, but Google+ pages can actually follow other Google+ profiles. This means that, in order to get noticed by your target demographic on Google+, you should be proactively circling them in hopes that they are attracted to your content. It's easy to do searches on Google+ to look for relevant consumers or people in your industry, such as potential partners, and then, just like you would create Twitter lists, you can categorize your circles and create different circles for different objectives. One might be for customers, another for competitors, and still another for thought leaders in your industry. It is public knowledge who you have in your circles and who has circled you, but how you label these circles is completely private, so categorize them in a way that makes strategic sense to you. You'll find that you can easily navigate through conversations via your circles, but you can also distribute content to specific circles based on your lists. If you have a following that spans different industries, you can create circles for each of them and share only relevant content to the relevant circles, which is something you can't do on any other social network. It's important to understand how relationships work on Google+ and create a variety of circles to optimize Google+ most effectively.

ABOUT PAGE

Creating a profile for your page is very easy, and the SEO is important. You have a title and a headline. Obviously, the name of your page should be the name of your company, and you should include keywords for your company in your tagline. Going further, after you fill in all the details and creative, the devil is in the details, because Google allows you to include a lot of additional information. This is critical; with this About page, you're telling Google about all the links that are important about your company on the Internet.

You have the ability to provide an introduction to your company, and you can customize the text and links here as well. It is critical to tell Google what is most important in this space. Showcase the top 10 or 20 pages of your website that you want to make sure Google indexes properly. Be liberal in the content and links you use. If you look at Mark Traphagen's posts and his about page,[5] you'll get an idea of what I'm talking about in terms of strategically linking to important web properties.

You can also link to all other digital assets, such as social media profiles and other blogs to which you contribute. If your company has a website or multiple websites, make sure you include links to all those, too. Use the About page to tell Google what you believe should be preferentially indexed for your company.

HANGOUTS

Every social network has its own unique functionality. In Google+, there are two: Circles and Hangouts, which basically allow 9 users and 1 host to have a video call in real time and interact with other users within the Google+ community. Similar to a Skype video call, this can be used in a variety of ways. If you're talking to someone in Google+ and you want to take it a step further, you can have a conversation with that person— or group of people—in a Google+ Hangout.

It is possible to use Hangouts for a variety of purposes, for which we are slowly seeing companies experiment with. Michael Dell, chairman and chief executive officer (CEO) of Dell, was one of the first to recognize the potential of using Hangouts for customer service shortly after they were introduced in 2011.[6] Since then, business use of Hangouts is still slow, but we've already seen the likes of Cadbury, Taylor Guitar, and small businesses use Hangouts for a variety of objectives.[7]

It should be noted that Hangouts can also be streamed publicly on your YouTube channel as well as your Google+ page through choosing the "Hangouts on air" option when you create your Hangout. Hangouts on air can be used similar to a webinar platform when you want to broadcast something to as wide an audience as possible, and because the recording of every Hangout on air is automatically saved to your YouTube account,[8] you've now created a digital asset as well.

Google Hangouts allow people to engage on a personal level through a video console that other platforms do not have. In general, businesses haven't really leveraged the potential here. Think creatively about how you might use this tool. There are many active communities on Google+, and you may find a lot of people talking about your brand or your industry. You may find that having a Google+ Hangout, similar to hosting a Twitter chat, may be an effective marketing tool for your company.

Similar to Twitter chats, the Google+ Hangout is the Holy Grail, and if you've optimized your Google+ presence to the greatest extent, you should experiment with Google+ Hangouts.

There is even more potential to create you own community on Google+ similar to creating a LinkedIn Group with the introduction of Google+ Communities.[9] Needless to say, with Google being the owner of Google+, you'll want to continue to keep an eye on the latest developments for this social platform to ensure that you continue to maximize your Google+ presence.

SPECIAL REPORT: HOW GOOGLE+ IS CHANGING THE ONLINE WORLD AND WHAT YOU CAN DO ABOUT IT

Google+ is one of the least used and even less understood yet most important social media channels. To help extend upon this chapter and put the social network into its proper perspective, I called upon the person I believe has the deepest understanding of Google+ to explain how it affects your online presence. Google+ contributor to Maximize Social Business, Mark Traphagen, provides this special report about how Google+ is truly changing the online world with concise and practical advice on how to adapt and use this online platform for your company's full benefit.

GOOGLE+ AND YOUR SEO, BY MARK TRAPHAGEN

When marketers and businesses first began to pay attention to social media, they tended to see it as a separate channel unto itself. Social media was all about engagement and customer relations. Search was the realm of SEO and was focused on driving traffic to a website. Only a few visionaries believed that one would ever have much to do with the other.

That began to change when it became apparent that search engines such as Google were actually interested in social media as a source of both content and meaningful signals on what should rank higher in search results. For a while, Google even displayed real-time tweets on its home page for fast-breaking, trending topics. The one thing Google lacked was a viable social network of its own.

Then came Google+.

Most people who have at least a rudimentary understanding of both SEO and Google+ will tell you that Google+ is important for SEO. They just usually don't know why that is so or what to do about it.

The truth is that Google+ can and does affect Google search in powerful ways. This platform has a powerful effect on Google search, not just because Google+ is a Google product, but because of the way Google+ is constructed. Google+ represents far more than Google's attempt to get into the social network race to compete with sites like Facebook and Twitter. The head of Google+, Vic Gundotra, has said, "It's really the unification of all of Google's services, with a common social layer."[10]

Google+ provides a direct benefit to Google, as it vastly enriches the data Google has from Google users. As people create profiles and then use the web while remaining signed in to Google, the platform can easily track and tie their identity information to their interests. Google gets even more such data when people actually use Google+, whether by simply +1'ing things across the web or more actively sharing and engaging on the network. These data enable Google to better personalize and target organic search results and advertising for users. Google knows that the better ads and results are targeted, the more responsive to them people are likely to be. Personalization also increases user satisfaction with Google, causing people to be more likely to use Google again.

Google+ and Social Signals

For businesses, the intention of Google to use Google+ to improve search results creates a powerful opportunity. Google+ is an open invitation by Google to help determine what should have prominence in a Google search. In part, this is due to the importance of social signals to search engines. Because social networks are populated by real people indicating what they like and think through their sharing, liking, retweeting, and +1'ing, it's only natural that search engines watch these signals.

Although use of social signals is still in its infancy, Google and Bing have both indicated they will only increase in importance in the coming years.[11]

Google+ and Web Influence

The most apparent effect on search is seen in Google personalized search. When a user is signed in to his or her Google+ account, that person's search results are influenced by people cataloged in his or her Google contacts. This means that the larger your Google+ network is, the more people whose search results are either directly or indirectly influenced by you.

(*continued*)

(*continued*)

Other Google+-related features that can help build online influence and branding include Google Authorship, which helps more people connect with all the content you produce, and the rel=publisher connection for brands, which can lead to a prominent Google Knowledge Graph display for your company's brand in a search.

Google+ and PageRank

All of those things are interesting, but the most important thing to know about Google+ and SEO is that Google treats Google+ profiles, brand pages, and communities just like regular websites when it comes to search. That only really hits home when you understand that Google+ profiles and pages have PageRank. (Twitter profiles do as well, but because of Google's lack of access to Twitter's full stream and the fact that most Twitter links are "no-follow" [they pass no PageRank "juice"], the amount of influence Twitter has on Google search is debatable.)

That's right: when it comes to search authority (and the ability to pass that authority along to others), Google+ profiles can be just as powerful as any other web page. That means you not only should be using Google+ for SEO but should be using it to do SEO.

PageRank of Google+ profiles and pages is important because, all other things being equal, web pages with a higher PageRank will generally rank better than pages with a lower PageRank for the same search term. Moreover, high-PageRank pages pass on more authority to the sites to which they are linked.

How Do Google+ Profiles Gain PageRank?

As with anything regarding the Google search algorithm, the answer is complex and there is much we don't know. Google keeps the secret sauce secret on purpose: if too much is known about how the algorithm ranks pages, webmasters would be very tempted to use that information to game the system. Nevertheless, we do know quite a bit about how PageRank works and how it is gained or lost by web pages. It is reasonable to assume that Google+ profiles and pages gain their PageRank the old-fashioned way: by links from authoritative web pages.

Google+ profiles most likely have another source of gaining PageRank: other Google+ profiles. Google can obviously see in great detail which profiles interact with other profiles. In the case of Google+, the equivalent of a web link from another profile might be that profile sharing one of your posts, or +mentioning you in a post. In this scenario, a link from a high-PageRank profile would build your profile's PageRank.

There may be other ways in which Google assesses the PageRank of a Google+ page or profile, but at this point, this is the base of what is commonly known.

What Are the Characteristics of High-PageRank Google+ Profiles?

After a careful study of high-PageRank Google+ profiles in comparison to my personal profile, I feel confident about the following conclusions:

- **It's not how many you know; it's who you know**. Higher-PageRank profiles tend to have active relationships with other high-PageRank profiles. In many cases, that's probably how they got their high PageRank. In my early days on Google+, I managed to attract the attention and respect of some top Google+ users. They began recommending me to others and sharing my posts. Within six months I discovered my profile ranked very well in search results.
- **Just following or being followed is not enough**. Some have mistakenly assumed that merely having a high-authority person in their circles, or being circled by them, is enough to have authority rub off on their profile. This is no truer than the idea that living in the same neighborhood as a famous person would make one famous. There must be interaction with the high-authority person for any authority to be passed; specifically, this person needs to share your content or mention your profile or page.
- **Backlinks are the backbone**. Just as with regular web pages, having a good number of links to your profile or brand page from authoritative web pages can build the PageRank and search authority of your profile or page. This means that it is just as important to be attracting good links to your profile as it is to build a powerful network within Google+. (Google Authorship automatically builds such backlinks if the author publishes on high-authority sites.)
- **Google+ PageRank can come from Google+ relationships, links from the web, or both**. In studies we've run of profiles at all levels of PageRank, we've seen a strong correlation between the strength of backlink profiles (the number and authority of links to a particular profile) and the PageRank of those profiles. But, and this is important, there are outliers and anomalies, profiles with very few or even no outside backlinks that still have high PageRank. It seems that the PageRank for those profiles must come entirely from their interactions on Google+, so you can use one or the other to build the authority of your page or profile. Obviously, a good combination of the two would have the most powerful effect.

(continued)

(continued)

What Is the Value of a High-PageRank Google+ Profile or Page?

The value of a high-PageRank Google+ profile or brand page runs in two directions:

1. **Posts from high-PageRank profiles usually rank better in search**. Google indexes public Google+ posts for search, and it appears they are ranked much in the same way regular web pages are. There is one important difference that makes having high PageRank for your profile even more important: Google tends to rank only a few (and often only one) Google+ post in a search for a given search term. When a keyword is hot on Google+, it is common for several posts to rank on the first page or two of Google search. But once things cool down, often only one or two remain that high, and those are almost always from high-authority profiles.

2. **Links from high-PageRank profiles to web pages are more valuable than links from lower- or no-PageRank profiles**. All links in Google+ posts used to be "dofollow" (meaning they passed on PageRank authority to whatever content they linked), but now only the "featured link" of a post is followed by Google. This is the link created when someone either shares a post to Google+ directly from a web page using the +1 button or when someone pastes the URL of a page into the link box in the Google+ share box. Such links are turned into a rich snippet at the bottom of the post (with an image from the post, its title in bold, and an excerpt). This emphasizes the importance of having a Google+ +1 button on all web and blog pages, because whenever a high-PageRank profile shares your post, an authoritative backlink to your web page is being created, and that increases your post's own search authority.

How to Build the SEO Power of Your Google+ Profile or Page

Based on what we've observed, I suggest the following strategies to build the search authority of your Google+ profiles and brand pages:

1. Continually create and share high-quality content on Google+ that demonstrates your level of expertise in your field.
2. Build relationships with others on Google+ who are influential in your field. As they begin to see you as a useful and helpful authority, they will share your content and recommend you, creating connections that will build your authority.

3. Pursue opportunities to earn links to your profiles and pages from authoritative web pages.

Expanding on the second point, here are some suggestions for building links to your Google+ profiles and pages:

1. Make note of those social media sites that allow a dofollow link in your profile. Here is a list of some of those sites: http://www.niceblogger .net/20-social-media-sites-offering-dofollow-profile-links/. You might want to consider making your Google+ profile your hub link for such profiles.
2. Include a profile link wherever possible in guest posts you write for other sites.
3. Use Google Authorship,[12] which always creates a link back to your profile.
4. Connect your website to your Google+ brand page with a verified rel=publisher connection.[13]
5. Have a Google+ +1 button displayed prominently on all your site content, encouraging visitors to share it to their Google+ streams, which creates PageRank-passing links back to your site.
6. Frequently publish blog-quality or newsworthy content directly from your profile or brand page. In addition to the Google+ reshares this will attract, websites and blogs that find the content interesting can link to it directly. (You can grab the direct URL of any Google+ post by right-clicking on its time stamp.)
7. Keeping the fifth point in mind, share posts from Google+ to social media and news sites just like you would share posts from your blog.

Source: Mark Traphagen[14] is director of social media marketing for Virante.[15] A former teacher, Mark has worked directly in Internet marketing since 2005, but he has been involved in social media and online community formation since the mid-1990s.

Chapter 11   Maximizing Visual Social Networks

To this point, we've concentrated on the major networks that are a part of most social strategies, or at least part of what most people participate in—blogs, Facebook, Twitter, LinkedIn, and Google+—but there are obviously a lot of other social media platforms available.

Does this mean you need to be involved in all platforms? Absolutely not. Your social media channel usage should be completely aligned with your social media strategy, which we covered back in Chapter 5.

In this chapter, we'll look at maximizing YouTube, Pinterest, and Instagram, channels that you may or may not be using depending on your target audience, your industry, and other factors. Some of these platforms may be more strategic for your company than others. For example, Pinterest is a natural fit for e-commerce, whereas Instagram is a great platform for engaging with mobile users as well as having crowdsourced photo campaigns. YouTube may also deserve your atten-tion because video is an important part of marketing, and the site is still considered the second largest search engine in the world.

VISUAL SOCIAL MEDIA MARKETING

Visual social media marketing platforms have became particularly popu-lar recently, and my 2013 prediction for the Content Marketing Institute[1] was that they will continue to be so:

> Although we have seen it emerging throughout 2012, 2013 will be the year in which content marketers truly embrace visual content. Whether it's always posting with an image to defeat EdgeRank on Facebook, creating an infographic to lure visitors in on Pinterest or crowdsourcing hashtagged photos on Instagram as part of a campaign, an important trend in content marketing in 2013 will be all about leveraging visual content.[2]

Before learning more on how to maximize your Pinterest, Instagram, and YouTube accounts, let's take a step back and dive deeper into this trend. To better understand the growing importance of visuals in social media marketing, I called upon Maximize Social Business's contributor for social media and content marketing, Bob Geller, to offer his analysis and advice on how you can best maximize your visual.

LEVERAGING THE VISUAL IN YOUR SOCIAL MEDIA MARKETING, BY BOB GELLER

There is no truer saying these days than "a picture speaks a thousand words." Pictures and other forms of visual content have become an increas-ingly important part of the social media marketer's arsenal, and there are a number of reasons for this.

The most important relates to something author Doug Rushkoff called narrative collapse in his book *Present Shock*.[3] Narrative collapse is what happens when we are stuck in the present: a social media, 24-hour cable news, sensory overload–driven *Groundhog Day* kind of reality. The constant onslaught of text messages, social network chatter, and other blaring media distracts us and robs us of our capacity to take time, process information, and put things into context. This makes it more difficult for social media teams, advertisers, and publishers to break through, engage people, and build audience.

In parallel with this trend has been the rise over the past few years of social media platforms and networks that are designed specifically for sharing visual information. Marketers are increasingly turning to sites such as Pinterest, Tumblr, Instagram, YouTube, and SlideShare and using visual content in their campaigns. The right imagery and sharing mechanism can give campaigns that extra juice needed to rise above the noise. Visual content can be used to pull people in, entertain, and communicate complex information in an easy-to-understand way. It offers a nice diversion in a busy social media environment. The right image can bypass our filters, trigger feelings and emotions, and put people in a buying mood. Visual content can be a powerful way to support and communicate brand attributes, as well as drive engagement.

This is why visual content such as images and videos, and the platforms on which they are published, should be key components of your social media marketing campaigns.

Writer's Block: Why Isn't It Easy to Put Images to Work?

Images are a welcome change among all the noise found in social media, and, let's face it: viewing can be more fun than reading. Yet, it is not necessarily easy to put images to work in an effective way. Brains or beauty? Left brain or right? Words or images? For as long as marketing has been around, there's been a tension between the use of words and pictures. This probably has something to do with silos and the way we function. Few people are great at both design and writing. Pictures take many marketers out of their copy-centric comfort zones. Fortunately, in most cases, you can use both words and images, although one usually needs to take center stage.

Although using imagery may involve unfamiliar skill sets, a look at the psychology of web marketing may convince you about its benefits. According to the online site ClickZ[4]:

> The instinctual reptilian brain can exert a powerful influence over both emotion and logic. [It] responds rapidly to visual cues. First impressions are always based on appearances, not information, and in the buying process, words are secondary to visual cues.

(continued)

(*continued*)

If images of dinosaur brains don't sway you to use imagery in marketing, perhaps cold hard logic and numbers will. At the end of 2012, TechCrunch[5] reported that Pinterest, a visual content sharing site, was the fourth largest traffic driver in the world.

Follow Professional Design Principles and Heed Basics in Image Usage

Although there certainly is a place for user-generated content, in most cases you want to have an edge by using professional-quality images and artwork. Get help from the pros if you don't have the talent in-house to produce the needed images. Don't necessarily rely on stock photography.

You also need to keep in mind some other basic things, such as steering clear of overly large images that take too long to load, frustrating users. Avoid making your images too complicated; infographics are supposed to paint a pretty and easy-to-understand picture about complex information, but sometimes they do just the opposite.

Also, when you are using third-party images, take care not to skirt copyright laws, such as what Maximize Social Business contributor Michelle Sherman touched upon in her post[6] "To Pin or Not To Pin: How Businesses Can Use Pinterest and Reduce Their Legal Risks of Copyright Infringement."

Fit Images into an Integrated Content Marketing Strategy and System

When done right, content and social media marketing employ images not just to grab attention but also to engage and coax the reader down a path that hopefully results in some type of meaningful business action, such as a sales conversion. Make sure the images you use support the greater effort and have a specific place and function in the overall system.

Source: Bob Geller[7] is president of Fusion PR[8] and has a background that combines a solid grounding in technology with a 25-year record of success in sales, marketing, and public relations. Bob joined Fusion in 2000 and has helped build it into a leading independent tech PR agency.

YOUTUBE

When creating a social media strategy, YouTube is often forgotten as being one of the most popular social media websites that exists. The ability to upload video to your channel and express your brand using a unique format has proved to be a powerful one for many brands small and large. Although not every video you create will become a viral smash, just looking at the success of companies such as Blendtec,[9] Orabrush,[10] and Gillette[11] gives you an idea of the potential for the strategic use of video as part of your social media strategy. Understanding the potential that YouTube might have for your business first begins with realizing the potential search engine optimization (SEO) benefits that a YouTube presence can provide you.

SEO

The statistics regarding YouTube above and beyond the fact that it is the second largest search engine in the world are incredible; the amount of content being shared and viewed is mind-boggling. Four billion videos are viewed each day. One Internet user watches an average of one YouTube video per day. Seventy-two hours of video is uploaded every minute.[12]

Best of all, all content on YouTube is indexed by Google. Because YouTube is owned by the social media giant, the title, description, and tags for video uploads play into how a video ranks in its search engine results. In fact, the real estate on the first page of Google results is being infiltrated by Google videos even when the search query isn't necessarily seeking a video. By creating compelling videos and using the right keywords in the accompanying text, your company could potentially rank higher for a video than it would for content on a website using the same terms.

Virality

SEO isn't the only benefit of using YouTube. The platform also has special perks and benefits.

- People love to watch and share video, so there's always a viral aspect that content may be amplified.
- People are social on YouTube, with 100 million people taking a social action (like, share, comment, etc.) on the platform every week.[13]

As an example of the how social media helps amplify your YouTube videos, consider that autoshared tweets[14] result in six new YouTube.com sessions on average. What this means is that when you create a video and allow YouTube to automatically share it on your behalf on Twitter through an automated tweet, on average your video will get six more YouTube views.

YouTube is a popular place to be, and it's very virally oriented. The creation of YouTube content has the potential to amplify a message into new areas.

Embed

When you upload a video to YouTube, you can embed it on your website and other social media profiles. In addition to embedding corporate videos on web pages, you can also use YouTube to embed videos on blog posts, and these don't have to be your own videos. Any authoritative videos from third parties make your blog a more reliable and trusted resource. Curate YouTube videos just like you would with other forms of content.

The ultimate goal is to make your website a good resource. If your blog posts are interesting and the embedded videos are relevant, people are more likely to spend more time on your website, which increases the chances you'll be able to convert them. This also lets Google know that your site has quality content because people are spending more time on it.

Don't forget that YouTube videos that you create might also be embedded on someone else's website. That's why it's always important when creating videos that you produce content that others would want to share.

Analytics

Similar to Facebook, YouTube also has an analytics dashboard to help you understand how your videos are doing in order to look for clues as to how you can improve upon them in the future.

There are a few specific statistics that are very helpful for understanding a YouTube video's performance, and you should consider adding them to your other YouTube metrics to analyze number of subscribers, video views, comments, and favorites. Listed in order from top to bottom where they currently appear on your YouTube dashboard, they are:

- **Playback location:** If your videos are being embedded in other websites, that information will appear here under "Embedded player on other websites" in the playback location column. Unfortunately, specific URLs for the embedded pages do not appear, but from a domain-level perspective you can see how your videos perform when shared on social platforms in addition to other websites that embed your videos.
- **Traffic locations:** As a search engine, similar to analyzing which keywords brought visitors to your website through Google Analytics, you can glean the exact same information to see which keywords brought YouTube search queries to watch your video by selecting "YouTube" search in the traffic source column.
- **Audience retention:** This tells you the average time in minutes and seconds that viewers spent watching each video as well as the percentage of the video that they actually watched. Also, a graph shows at what point people stopped watching the video. This is helpful advice that can be used to create better, more engaging videos. Use this statistic to see what the video contained at that specific point in time to figure out why people clicked away. Compare this with videos with higher retention and those that weren't as engaging.
- **Subscribers:** Which videos prompted more YouTube users to subscribe to your channel? The answer is here!
- **Sharing:** This tells you which of your videos received the most social shares. Part of maximizing your social is in creating shareable content, so ideally you want to create videos that are shared in social media. This is one direct statistic you can monitor to see if you've met that goal and to determine how popular your videos are.

Video marketing is one of the most time- and labor-intensive forms of marketing, and for companies that are just beginning social media marketing, video requires the biggest investment. Nonetheless, video is an important component to maximizing your social media presence, although it may be more appropriately instituted as part of a phased approach and integrated into the marketing mix at a later time. If you find, however, that using video is a smart strategic move for your company, it may be worth the investment in time and budget early in the social media strategy.

STRATEGIC YOUTUBE MARKETING

Because YouTube is an often forgotten yet strategic platform, I wanted to offer a little more advice from a YouTube expert to help you truly maximize your YouTube presence, so I have invited my social media and video contributor for Maximize Social Business, Jayson Duncan, to provide further insight on this important subject.

HOW TO LEVERAGE VIDEO AND INCREASE YOUR SOCIAL MEDIA PRESENCE WITH YOUTUBE MARKETING, BY JAYSON DUNCAN

When it comes to social media, the power of online video is undeniable. Video creates a personal connection in a way text can't. It seems that most businesses are catching on to that fact, yet every once in a while, I still find myself in a meeting with an executive who insists his target market doesn't watch online video.

Forbes magazine recently released an article that reported that 75 percent of executives watch work-related videos[15] at least weekly, and more than half of those watch work-related video on YouTube.[16]

Many marketers disregard YouTube as a mere extension of the show *America's Funniest Home Videos*,[17] but the fact is, YouTube has grown up over the past few years. It is more than a place to store your videos; it is a social media platform, and it has the ability to level the playing field for companies that want to start a conversation with clients and customers using video. There are many video sharing sites out there, but for social media purposes, YouTube should be at the top of your strategy plan.

How do you start using video as part of your social media marketing strategy? Create a programming schedule frequency, just like you would for your favorite TV show. If you are going to create content, plan to do it once a week and release it the same day and time every week so people know when to tune in.

If you can't create video once a week, how about shooting for once a month? If this sounds daunting, record several on the same day and release them over time. This also gives you content for your blog, something to tweet, and something to share on Facebook. You can create tent pole programing, which means creating a special video around holidays such as Christmas or Mother's Day. This has worked well in the TV world. *A Charlie Brown Christmas* was first aired in 1965, and people still gather around each year to watch it.

YouTube is a community, just like other social media platforms. It takes time to connect with other users to help build your YouTube viewership and subscribers.

YouTube has placed more importance on subscribers in the past few months. You need to interact and not just post. Be sure to like others' videos, subscribe to their channels, and comment on their videos. You can even use videos to respond to their videos. Old Spice used the power of engagement[18] in the follow-up to its "Your Man Can Smell Like" videos. This created 180 video responses. They received 5.9 million YouTube views in the first day of launch. Although your company may not have the resources for this type of campaign, the point is they used video to engage viewers.

One trap that companies fall into is thinking that because this video is published online, it doesn't have to be good. That might have been true in the early days of YouTube but that is no longer the case. The only amateur content that is considered acceptable is user-generated content. There are exceptions to this, but if you are a professional company with amateur marketing, viewers may feel like you don't care about them.

There are many different types of videos that will work as part of your social media marketing strategy. Here are a few:

- **Video blogs:** Post this video to YouTube and then post it to your blog. Blogs with video have an increased view rate. You can also use YouTube to drive viewers to your blog.
- **Testimonial videos:** Make your product or service visible and credible. When you say something yourself, it is bragging, but when someone else says it about you, it is fact. Use this to your advantage and help viewers picture themselves enjoying your product or service. It also helps people relate to your company.
- **Training or how-to videos:** Answer questions people have and help viewers feel like they have received value from your company. This is also true of videos that answer frequently asked questions.
- **Company overview:** This is one video I think all companies can benefit from by giving a face to the company and telling the company story.[19]

The bottom line is that video content is easier than ever to create, but creating good content is an art that requires strategic planning and professional effort. Good video content with a good picture and sound is an investment of time and money that will provide strong return on investment for your social media marketing strategy.

Source: Jayson Duncan[20] is an Orange County, California, filmmaker and owner of the video production company Miller Farm Media.[21] In 2003, Jayson began using video to help others tell their stories through his video production company, which has now created videos for a variety of businesses, including Fortune 50 companies.

PINTEREST

Similar to Google+ and Instagram, Pinterest came out of nowhere and in the past year and a half it has blossomed into a major platform. Pinterest is important for many reasons, but the main reason is simply because it's so popular. It is currently the fifteenth most visited website in the United States and thirty-fourth in the world.[22] It has a high number of very active users, with early data showing the average time spent on Pinterest being more than the average time spent on LinkedIn, Twitter, and Google+ combined.[23] The site's unique functionality and demographics may make it an important social platform for your company.

Referral Power

Pinterest is sending more referral website traffic to other sites than Yahoo!, Bing, or Twitter. According to some statistics, it is second only to Facebook in terms of social referral traffic.[24] This means a lot of people are clicking on content on Pinterest and then going to another website. Because it's become a reliable source of referral traffic, it has great potential for your company.

Because of the mechanics of the platform, if you want to drive traffic to your website, Pinterest is a natural fit. A photo or video can be pinned directly to a board, or images from websites can be added to a pin board. When another Pinterest user clicks on a pin that they see added from your website, Pinterest sends them directly to your site.

For e-commerce sites that have lots of pages with images of products, Pinterest is a good way to maximize social marketing, because it has the potential to direct traffic right to your site. Several e-commerce sites have been very successful with this strategy, with clothing retailers seeing the earliest benefit.[25]

The following case studies of those companies that are already seeing success on Pinterest highlight its potential:

- **Indigo,** Canada's largest book, gift, and specialty toy retailer, integrated a Pinterest button on their website and two months later, in addition to a number of other amazing statistics, Pinterest jumped to represent 40 percent of their traffic from social media. This also helped social referral traffic in total to grow by 218 percent, no doubt helped by Pinterest users being able to easily share pins to Facebook and Twitter.[26]

- **Sony Electronics** in the United States took time to research what others were pinning before deciding to launch their Pinterest presence. They launched in strategic fashion by involving their own employees as well as cross-promoting their Pinterest presence on their other social media channels. The result six months later was an 800 percent increase in traffic from Pinterest to the Sony Store and more than 4 million brand impressions.[27]

- **Camiband** is a clothing accessory for women started by a husband and wife team. They were fortunate when their product was introduced on-air on national television, generating 3,500 visits to their website. A few months later, a Pinterest user's pin of their product from their site went viral, generating 40,000 website visits in four days from Pinterest alone—and sparking a sharp increase in sales.[28]

Lucrative Demographic

Just as people use Google when they are researching a product or service they may want to buy, Pinterest is used for visual inspiration. Users will create boards full of future purchases, ideas, and inspiration, and creators of those boards as well as other Pinterest users use those boards to shop online. They look for websites selling the items they want to purchase, and companies carrying those products and services satisfy that need. When users pin your items, they create visual shopping lists—and your items may be among those they want to buy.

Pinterest users make up a lucrative demographic group. They make purchases at rates that those on other social media network platforms do not. One study shows that the average purchase from a Pinterest user is higher than the average Facebook and Twitter user purchase price combined.[29] Beauty products retailer Sephora found that Pinterest users spent 15 times more than Facebook users did.[30]

Pinterest is primarily fueled by female consumers.[31] Some analysts believe that because women often manage the household budget, it can help explain why the Pinterest demographic seems to be more lucrative than others. Pinterest attracts buyers, and if a target demographic in your social media strategy is primarily women, this is where your company needs to be.

Virality of Pins

Pinterest users are not just pinning content; they're repinning others' content at an incredibly high rate. Pinterest is a very virally oriented platform, and 80 percent of Pinterest pins are actually repins from other boards.[32] This means a lot of people are looking at boards and repinning content other users have already found.

To maximize your presence on Pinterest and leverage the viral nature of the platform, you need to create pinnable content that is visually oriented. It needs to attract the first pinner and be attractive to all of his or her friends. In addition to creating content others would want to share, building a community of relevant followers on Pinterest, as well as timing the posting of your photos to when your target demographic is primarily using the site, will increase your chances of receiving repins for your content.

Optimize Your Pinterest Presence

Now that you see the potential that Pinterest might have for your social media strategy, you'll need to set up boards on Pinterest for your pinning. To integrate Pinterest fully into your content strategy, the boards should be aligned with your content buckets. In addition to the description to your boards, you'll also want to ensure that any pin that you add includes a keyword-rich description. You then want to add Pinterest engagement into your daily routine, both pinning new and legacy photos from your website over time as well as curated photos from the Pinterest community in order to both satisfy your content curation as well as engagement needs. Pinterest recently added analytics after you verify your website with them to give you a better view as to the referral traffic your pins are generating, so use that data to help optimize your pinning as part of the recommended PDCA approach to your social media implementation. Finally, as the earlier case studies indicated, don't forget to add Pinterest buttons to all pages, services, and products that have relevant images on your website.

Pinterest Campaigns

Once you've optimized your Pinterest as I recommended and are growing a larger Pinterest community and seeing increased website traffic, it's time to consider your first Pinterest campaign. Campaigns can be just as successful on Pinterest as they are on other social media platforms. Pinterest has its own search engine that helps people find content, so it's an ideal platform for campaigns because users can become directly involved with your content and pin your pins to their own boards as part of the campaign.

There have been many unique and successful campaigns in Pinterest's short history worth noting, but unfortunately most of them would not be allowed under Pinterest's new guidelines[33] because they required users to pin from a selection, requested others to pin or repin the contest rules, ran a sweepstakes-like competition, asked participants to comment, required a minimum number of pins, or asked pinners to vote with pins, repins, boards, or likes. Therefore, going forward a best practice is to run a campaign asking users to pin an image from your website based around a common theme using a branded keyword as the way to judge entrants that you find through a Pinterest search.

Although Pinterest offers a great campaign platform, make sure that you are aware of its current rules in detail.[34] There are some hoops to jump through but it may be beneficial if you want to leverage the visual opportunities offered by your products and services by this potentially lucrative social platform.

Pinterest might not be the most appropriate channel for every social media strategy, but if you are selling a product to consumers that has visual appeal as well as a natural fit into one of Pinterest's search categories (revealed by hovering over the three-line icon in the upper left-hand corner), you should definitely include this platform as part of your social media strategy.

INSTAGRAM

Instagram is also an emerging platform worth exploring for your social media strategy. Instagram is unique in that it is the first major social platform based on mobile. It already has more than 100 million users, has been bought out by Facebook, and although there is a website component, is primarily used from a smartphone or a smart device (like an iPad). With the world awaiting further integration between Instagram and Facebook and the growing popularity of smartphones as well as the camera functionality on them, Instagram is a social platform that is well positioned for future growth.

Brand Awareness

What is the use of Instagram from a social media marketing perspective? A lot of companies struggle with this. They see the potential with other platforms—Google+ has a distinct SEO advantage, Pinterest offers a link back to the company's website, so there is a direct potential click through return on investment—but Instagram remains a mystery. With this platform, users can publish a photo with content, and although you can include a URL in the content area, it isn't a clickable link. However, there are still benefits to using Instagram.

In listing the objectives for using social media, many companies note that brand awareness is one of their goals. If you want to build brand awareness and your product or service is likely to have mobile users, Instagram can help you connect with its users who are all using mobile devices. You can also use this platform to make a splash with your target demographic group if they are active on Instagram, which data suggest might currently have the youngest user base of any major social platform.[35]

There are already companies that have reaped the business benefits of increased brand awareness to Instagram users. The owner of ShopExcessBaggage.com, a women's online retailer that has gained more than 100,000 followers[36]—and business—from Instagram, was quoted as saying,

> Every image we post is like a virtual billboard in Times Square. I've used all the social media tools out there to help support my business but none have had the direct impact on sales that Instagram has had.[37]

Hashtag Campaigns

The hashtag was originally developed on Twitter as a way to classify tweets but has become a classifier for anything and everything from TV shows to consumer brand taglines to Twitter chats. Now it's jumped platforms and has been embraced by Instagram.

In Instagram, hashtags are the primary tool used for campaigns. With an Instagram campaign, users often need to upload their photos and tag them using a predetermined hashtag in order to get involved. Their followers then see that hashtag and, if they are interested, can click on it to find out more about the campaign and your brand. Instagram search fully supports hashtags, similar to Twitter.

Taking it one step further, because every hashtag on Instagram automatically has an RSS feed associated with it,[38] you can display those photos from your contest on your website or a Facebook app. You can use campaigns to crowdsource the visuals of what people think about your products or services and then integrate your fans' photos into your digital properties for everyone to see. The result is making your followers feel like they are a part of your brand.

Another aspect about Instagram campaigns that is important is that because most smartphones now have high-resolution cameras, using Instagram lets people take photos on the go and quickly upload them as part of a campaign. This strategy can be used anytime to show off your products or customers or promote relevant themes and can be particularly successful if it's used during a live event.

Maximize Your Visual

A study earlier this year showed that almost 60 percent of the Interbrand Top 100 Brands already had an Instagram account.[39] What was revealing about this study, though, is that 98 percent of photos posted were also shared to Facebook, which resulted in an average Facebook engagement per photo of 274 actions. Although Twitter shares were lower, 59 percent of photos posted by these brands were also shared to their Twitter accounts, resulting in 22 tweets per photo. In other words, if you have visual content to share, sharing on Instagram is a convenient way to also post those same images to Facebook and Twitter. These data support that this is exactly what big brands are doing to maximize their visual content.

The other way of maximizing your visual on Instagram is to determine your visual strategy for the platform wisely. Although Pinterest provides a tactical way to allow your website images to attract traffic among its users, Instagram is more about making noise with your images and visually standing out in the community. This is why tactics used by many successful brands on Instagram include using your followers as models from fan submissions, showing off your products in a uniquely creative way, providing behind-the-scenes shots at events, or providing followers with only the best of your images.

Because Instagram is relatively new, there is a lot of opportunity to experiment with the platform and figure out how it works best for your company. Try following some of this advice and experiment to ascertain how your business can best maximize your Instagram.

Social media is in a constant state of flux, and what is popular today may fall off the radar tomorrow. We've seen the rise and fall of popular platforms such as MySpace and social bookmarking sites like Digg and StumbleUpon. As part of the never-ending experimentation inherently built into social media, if the medium fits into your target strategy, it makes sense to use it in order to maximize your social media presence. Some of the social platforms noted in this chapter may have received minimal mention compared with Facebook at this point in time, but keep an eye on these and other emerging sites that have the potential to develop over time.

Chapter 12   Determining Staffing Roles and Responsibilities

By now, you've learned enough to create your social media strategy on the major social media platforms and efficiently maximize implementation of the strategy on all of them. However, for many companies creating social media strategies, there is one big problem: the person doing all this work is probably you.

There's a lot to be done with a social media strategy, but your company has to figure out how to create a social strategy that can actually be implemented. Instead of constantly trying to figure out what to say or do in social media on the spot, it is essential that organizations plan ahead by considering the roles and responsibilities necessary for successful implementation of social.

A number of strategies can be used to insource work and organize teams within an enterprise for social media purposes. Once your business begins to see the return on investment (ROI) of its social media activity, you'll better understand the evolution of how social media teams begin to be created within multiple departments of your company.

WHO'S GOING TO DO ALL THIS WORK?

Many types of people in a variety of roles can help with the social media strategy implementation. Based on my experience of working with other companies, as well as industry standards and case studies, I'd like to offer insight on a few of these roles.

Intern

Most companies fail at implementing their social media strategy because they hire interns to do the work for them. Once a social media strategy is created, it seems like it would be easier to manage interns by advising them of the set social media guidelines, and it is probably easier for interns who know exactly what they should and should not be doing in certain scenarios.

However, the problem is that most companies choose interns who are young and active social media users, but they're familiar with the space only from a personal perspective, not necessarily from a professional one. Many companies have regretted having hired social media interns to do the heavy lifting for them who then used questionable judgment. For example, one "overenthusiastic intern" from Habitat UK hijacked popular hashtags to promote its brand,[1] an intern at Red Cross bragged about getting "slizzered" on the company account,[2] and Chrysler's Twitter account handler released an expletive-laden slam to Detroit drivers.[3]

These companies may have put the brunt of the work on interns and probably let the interns do whatever they wanted to do. Implementing social media is not a technical job like coding with search engine optimization (SEO) in mind or creating a website. The person doing social media for your company is the voice of your brand to potentially hundreds of millions of social media users, so before you hire that intern, think twice.

However, if there is someone who can actively manage interns who work in social media, that may be a safer move. Companies can leverage interns, but it has to be done carefully; the interns should know your brand and your industry very well. Unfortunately, unless you are targeting the intern's demographic group, it may be hard to find the right fit.

Some companies, especially in business-to-business (B2B) industries, reach out to master's and PhD students who are studying in the same niche area. These people might be more invested and able to help more with content creation and curation than an intern who might not possess the same industry or product knowledge.

Shared Role

Many companies with a social media presence have a single person managing these online platforms while also balancing other responsibilities such as marketing, corporate communications, or public relations. Those in this position know that social media is time-intensive work, and other work may take priority over social. However, some might find they're more passionate about implementing the social media strategy, resulting in their other duties being delayed. Regardless, it is personally frustrating to try to manage all of this work at once; other managers may become frustrated as well, and the company at large may suffer.

Nonetheless, the shared role of social media with other work is probably the most practical and rational way to begin social media implementation. Until a company shows an ROI and illustrates the need for additional resources to the executive team, this may be the only option. But it needs to be done in a way where management understands that only x percent of time is spent on social media and a logical division of work exists on a day-to-day basis.

Because social media happens 24/7, it can be hard to manage this direct division of time, but sticking to a time schedule will be beneficial in many ways. For instance, a shared role allows for direct measurement of how much manpower and time are being invested in social media. A fixed schedule of x hours makes it easy to calculate the expense part of the ROI. It also becomes very clear to management that attention is being placed on other job duties but that social media is still addressed. This is often the best internal win-win solution.

There's no ideal way of implementing social media into a shared role. Depending on the primary role in the company and how much time can be spent on social media each day, success will differ. Those in a shared role should know they are not alone; many have come before, and many more will follow.

Dedicated Role

Having one person dedicated to the implementation, management, and optimization of the social media strategy is the ideal situation. This person becomes the social media lead for the company and is the go-to person for all things related to social media. When the company evolves from pure social media marketing to a social business, this person would train and help others with the transition.

A lot of smaller businesses wonder if they need to hire someone full-time to implement their social media plans. Not at the beginning, but there is no lack of content to create and tasks to complete for someone in this role. Most companies do not have large enough public relations or marketing teams to create a dedicated role, but innovative managers with enough resources who are interested in implementing social media in an ideal way have the most freedom by handing this role over to someone who is completely dedicated to it.

Sourcing Talent Internally

The sourcing of talent internally is a process of finding the right person who can eventually transition into holding the dedicated social media role. In my experience, most companies find this person from marketing, corporate communications, or public relations. However, other companies have been successful at insourcing talent from customer service.

Customer service people are normally fairly sociable people because they are used to dealing with clients. They are probably used to people with issues and are therefore good with handling and solving problems. They probably have a very deep understanding of a company's products, services, and customer base. They also know whom to speak to internally when they have a problem. These are all very important characteristics for the person who is handling social media.

When you consider insourcing talent, look to those customer-facing employees who have similar traits. In addition to these, look for someone who has the following traits:

- **Has corporate experience.** This person should have worked with your company or been in the industry a long time. If you are worried about age, remember that social media components are trainable, whereas industry knowledge and professional experience are not.
- **Is a team player.** This person will work with other divisions and multiple people within each division, as well as social media users.
- **Has strong communication skills.** This includes verbal and written communication.
- **Understands the customer.** This person should understand the average customer's demographics, interests, and habits.
- **Is passionately social.** This doesn't mean this person is a passionate user of social media but rather that this person is a passionately social person. This person shouldn't try to hide from people, although being an extrovert isn't required. Many successful social media managers I know are actually introverts.

Sourcing Content Internally

When you implement a social media strategy, the burden doesn't have to be on one person or even only your social media team. Implementing various components of a social media strategy varies in time consumption, and you'll likely find the type of work that requires the most time is content creation.

Because creating content can be time-consuming, harness those sources within your company who can help tell the company's story. Find people working internally who are truly passionate about the company or have an outward customer-facing role to put personality behind the brand. Invite people from all different departments to participate in the content creation, and you may find that an added advantage is the creation of a better, stronger internal company culture. All Nippon Airways in Japan is a good example of innovatively insourcing content for its Facebook page by taking photos and messages from employees.[4]

Although there are certainly things to avoid in terms of content creation, think creatively to find fresh and interesting ways to insource as much content from as many people within your company as possible. This strengthens your social media brand and will accelerate social media efforts. In time, your company will evolve into a true social business.

Outsourcing

I mention outsourcing last because I made a decision early in my career to help companies leverage social media from a strategic perspective and become an educator rather than do social media on others' behalf. There are plenty of technical and specialized tasks that make sense to outsource if you don't have internal resources, such as web design, SEO, or management of complex pay-per-click or limited-term advertising campaigns. Social media, on the other hand, is something that must lie as close to the heart of the brand as possible. Therefore, in an ideal world where internal resources exist, there is no need to outsource the work.

That said, just as your company might hire a social media intern, there are very efficient ways to outsource social media tasks when there are limited resources within the business. It may especially make sense to outsource some of those tasks if you're doing experimentation that increases the bandwidth for your social media program.

Don't outsource your social media strategy creation (unless you're working with a consultant like myself; obviously if I didn't believe in what I was saying, I wouldn't write it!). As long as you own the strategy and can ensure the outsourced solution follows your strategy, you can feel certain the agency is acting on your behalf just as if it were a part of your company. Finding a social media agency that would agree to work under these restrictions may not be easy, because every agency has its own rules and work styles. In order for you to implement your social media strategy efficiently, however, you must have any social media outsourcing company sign off on the strategy to ensure a higher chance of success. The agency must know the direction of your company, what your company wants to achieve with social media, and how to deliver tactically.

WHO'S IN CHARGE OF SOCIAL? EVERYONE.

Companies often have internal debates about who is in charge of the social media program before giving it a home. As your company evolves into a social business, there is no one department that truly owns its social media program. Chances are the eventual social media lead will sit in a department that controls the budget for a majority of these social media efforts. Understanding the uniqueness of social and removing internal politics from the equation will free up your entire company to embrace social. You'll be on your way to creating an inclusive internal culture with regard to social media, and this will help contribute to the success of implementing your social media strategy.

A survey by the leading social media advisory firm Altimeter shows that most businesses place social media in one of two departments—40 percent of those surveyed deemed it the responsibility of marketing, and 26 percent labeled it as corporate communications' responsibility.[5] With 66 percent of companies placing social media programs in these two departments, consider starting with these areas when you launch your social media program (if there isn't a particular social media division for it right now).

Remember, though, that this is only a starting point: there will be a need for social throughout the enterprise. Ask yourself and your internal department managers the same question I ask my consulting clients the first time I meet them: "Who are all of the potential internal stakeholders within the company who could be affected, might be presently using, or should be using social media?"

The answer to this question will often result in a list that includes many different departments. This is because social media likely began with either marketing, corporate communications, or public relations taking the lead, but somewhere along the road a recruiter in the human resources department or a salesperson decided he or she wanted to use it, too. To integrate all these needs into the website, information technology (IT) took on a role. With all these people involved in social media within the company, the legal department stepped in and decided a social media policy was needed. As time goes on, even more departments, including customer service and product development, will take an active role in social media.

This is the nature of social media—it touches everything. Even if your company is in the very beginning stages of integrating a social media strategy and only the public relations or marketing departments are involved, now is the time to consult with other departments to create a more complete social media strategy. By doing so, you'll find help in staffing roles and responsibilities, especially in the creation of in-house teams that you'll need in the future.

Organizing Internal Social Media Teams

Ultimately, your company needs to create multifunctional teams throughout the enterprise that can help in the operation, management, optimization, and internal reporting of the social media program. Task these social media teams with three different functions. I will give these teams names, but you'll want to make sure that they take on the nomen-clature that best fits your internal needs.

1. **Strategy team:** The strategy team, as the name implies, is in charge of the overall strategy behind the social media plan and ROI. If the person in charge of ROI of the social media plan is the social media lead, chief marketing officer, or vice president of marketing, that person should be managing the strategy team. The strategy team should also be made up of other influential stakeholders throughout the company's departments, but they shouldn't be so high up the chain of command that they are too far removed from the day-to-day operations of your social team.

   Ideally, those on the strategy team are those that are department heads or have strategic roles within the departments most involved with social media, such as customer service, marketing, and public relations. However, they shouldn't be the people actually implementing the strategy at a tactical level. They should steer the strategy and get reports from those involved with the day-to-day processes.

2. **Operations team:** This is made up of those people who are actually doing the social media work. In addition to the social media lead or shared role who is implementing or was the first to implement the D part of your PDCA social media strategy, there are others internally in different departments who are executing similar roles.

These people are in charge of fielding social media customer service inquiries, doing social recruiting, leveraging social for public relations, and looking for social media sales opportunities on various platforms.

Make sure those people who have hands-on contact with customers through social media are part of the operations team. This allows the operations team to understand what day-to-day issues the other team members are handling, allowing them to more easily strategize on how to address similar potential issues in the future. People on the operations team should meet regularly and share best practices so that they all can improve in their jobs and offer invaluable feedback based on shared experiences to the strategy team.

3. **Executive council:** The executive council encompasses all those executives to whom the strategy team reports. This also includes the person in charge of the ROI, someone who must be a part of this council. This is where reporting is delivered and executives share in the ownership of the company's social media strategy. It is on this council where you get executive buy-in. Executives need to become invested in what social media can do, and by having an executive council, this provides that opportunity, thus allowing internal teams to become better at what they do. The executive council might not frequently speak directly to the operations team, but it should be in conversation with the strategy steering team on a regular basis.

Organizing social media teams into these three segments and ensuring that there is regular communication inside them as well as frequent reporting from one team to another should help ensure that a social media strategy is properly staffed and implemented and that ownership is shared throughout the company. The larger the enterprise, the bigger and more important these teams will be.

YOUR FUTURE SOCIAL MEDIA ORGANIZATION

Eventually, social media touches nearly every department within a company. Outside of creating the cross-functional teams recommended in the prior section, how should you organize your entire organization around your social media efforts?

Altimeter's research[6] shows there are five common ways of internally organizing your social media efforts, so this is a good place to start thinking about your social media organization's design. The five models are decentralized, centralized, hub and spoke, multiple hub and spoke (dandelion), and holistic.

Although there are five different approaches, the top three most popular (according to the statistics as well as my own personal experience) are centralized, hub and spoke, and dandelion.

Centralized (29.1 Percent)

With a centralized organization, one department manages all the social media activities internally. By now, you probably realize this is where many companies start when they formalize their social media programs. If you are just embarking on your first social media strategy, this is probably where your company is at or is heading right now.

Although it seems rational at the beginning, the problem with this approach is that social media is a tool that overlaps everything else in your company. How can a marketing department that is in charge of social media manage the social media activities in customer service, IT, or other departments that are relevant to your brand? Those tasks should ideally be managed by people in those specific departments. That's why this department organization is normally an evolutionary phase to acquire social media experience before a company moves on to become a more social business.

Hub and Spoke (35.4 Percent)

This is very simple and works just like it sounds. According to Altimeter, the hub and spoke is a "cross-functional team [that] sits in a centralized position and helps various nodes such as business units."[7] These nodes can also be different departments. This is where the social media lead noted earlier is involved, but as a company's perspective on social media becomes more strategic, this will likely develop into an organization that we currently call a social media center of excellence.

Social media centers of excellence are cross-functional teams that are in a centralized location and internally serve the entire company. There are many early-adopter role models to learn from here. Some examples of companies that established centers of excellence include Intel, Adobe, Dell, and eBay.[8]

Dandelion (23.6 Percent)

This multiple hub-and-spoke organization is appropriate when you want to scale social media across different business units, brands, regional locations, or countries. This is where you have one global center of social media excellence working with other hub-and-spoke organizations. The central hub shares best practices, may manage other hubs, and makes sure there is some global unity within the brand through social media. This ensures the social media strategy is implemented the same way regardless of business unit, brand, or location.

One thing to consider is that your social media organization will naturally evolve as social media becomes a common task that most departments manage and eventually build their own expertise in. I had a chance to speak with Cory Edwards, director of social media for Dell,[9] about their evolutionary experience here. He points out that Dell, like most companies, began social media from a grassroots effort internally that then became centralized. Over time it made sense to move to a hub-and-spoke model, and now Dell's social media has gone decentralized to the point that it is completely integrated and distributed throughout the organization. The decentralized hub was recently disbanded so that each team member could be moved directly into relevant parts of the organization. The former hub now exists only as a virtual team comprised of social media headcount sitting across various areas of the business with a Social Media Leadership Council meeting regularly to ensure alignment. Although a hub-and-spoke model will satisfy the needs of companies early on in their social media journey, Dell's experience hints that at some point, there will be a need to ensure that every department is empowered and educated to implement social media on its own. This is the direction where I see most large businesses heading, and it serves as an excellent potential role model for your social media organization in the future.

Deciding who is going to spearhead the company's social media work, how to operate the social media plan internally, who will work on the plan internally, and how to structure the multifaceted work is at the heart of a successful social media strategy. As you begin to see the ROI of social media and scale your programs appropriately, your company will likely accelerate activity and these decisions will become more important. There is no right or wrong way in which to do this, but understanding basic organizational options ahead of time and how companies have evolved will help your company create and implement a social media strategy that works well into the future.

Chapter 13   Onboarding Your Social Media Strategy

Implementing your social media strategy successfully requires that your company create the right staffing roles and responsibilities and devise an inclusive social media culture through the use of effective internal communications involving the social media program and having social media guidelines that employees know and follow. Only then can the social media strategy you create become a true part of your company's culture.

CREATING AN INCLUSIVE SOCIAL CULTURE

If you've taken the advice in Chapter 12 and expanded your company's social media strategy to include stakeholders in all departments and created various teams to help oversee social efforts, you are well on your way to successfully expanding the use of social media throughout your company.

Create social media guidelines (covered in this chapter) and use your internal communications team to let everyone in the company know about the social media strategy. Make your social media organization—including the various teams discussed in Chapter 12—open and transparent to the entire company and, ideally, have top leadership deliver this message. If your company is too big or geographically distributed, create an internal video to disseminate this information.

Creating a truly inclusive social culture goes beyond making this announcement, though. Invite every single employee to become a part of your social media program and empower each with the ability to do so. Although I'm not suggesting that overnight you can become a company like Zappos, which is known for an open and trusting culture (some say the chief executive officer even forces employees to tweet on behalf of the company[1]), there are specific steps you can take to invite others internally to participate in your social media program to create a more inviting culture for your social initiatives and provide benefits for the entire organization as well:

- **Internally sourcing stories (and ideas):** The previous chapter briefly discussed the notion of internally sourcing talent as well as content. Create an internal channel—and regularly making an internal call to action—where employees can share their stories, whether long ones that can be repurposed into blog posts, short anecdotes that can provide the inspiration for tweets, or photos that can help your brand better maximize your Instagram. Don't just stop there. Because social media requires never-ending experimentation, openly welcome the creative ideas that your employees have about campaigns, platforms, or anything else about which they have passion. If possible, you might want to allow the idea creator to have a hand in guiding the implementation as well.

- **Utilizing employees as brand ambassadors:** If you're considering a brand ambassador program for your biggest fans, why wouldn't you include your employees in that program as well or create a similarly crafted one for them? By rewarding loyal and passionate employees just as you do your fans, you might be able to achieve similar amplification of content to a complimentary audience and help unleash passion toward your brand aimed at a trusted demographic in social media: friends of your employees.

- **Using employees as a formal extension of your social media team:** Similar to the notion of using your employees as brand ambassadors is having employees become an extension of the social media team. New platforms have been created that allow employees to opt in and share your messages with their community in a formalized way. For instance, you can ask your employees to opt in to a platform like Jobvite, which can help get the word out about new job openings by allowing your employees to easily share the news. Similarly, using a platform such as GaggleAMP can allow all of your employees to conveniently share your company's latest blog posts and social media updates with their personal networks. In such a way, you can formally activate the potential of your internal employees to help spread the word for your company, and hopefully you will have helped provide value to them and their networks, too.

Social media has the potential to strengthen your company culture because it is a medium in which everyone can truly participate. By allowing everyone in your company an equal chance to participate in the social media program, you have the opportunity to create a stronger culture in which everyone has a social voice that benefits the company.

As you begin to implement your social media strategy, there will be a need to raise the digital IQ of all of your employees in order to help the company truly leverage the potential for your social media strategy company-wide. Because of this, internal guidelines should be developed to provide employees with direction somewhere between the social media strategy you create and the legal restrictions outlined in a lawyer-approved social media policy (to be covered in Chapter 14). This document is called Social Media Guidelines, and although most companies have likely created such a document, it may be time to take a fresh look at it in light of the newly created social media strategy. For this reason, I invited veteran public relations and communications professional and Maximize Social Business contributor Joel Don to provide his insight.

THE IMPORTANCE OF—AND HOW TO CREATE—SOCIAL MEDIA GUIDELINES FOR YOUR EMPLOYEES, BY JOEL DON

Without a doubt, the most effective social media strategy for any company or organization will enlist every employee as a supportive extension of the social media marketing team. Earlier in this chapter, you learned about the importance of creating an *inclusive* social media culture at your company and why successful businesses actively encourage their employees to enthusiastically participate in social media channels. A social media marketing program works best when traditional corporate hierarchies and the turf battles created by departmental silos are abandoned in favor of a flat organizational structure that values and nurtures the involvement of all employees. But in this democratized social media world, we still have rules to follow. A separate chapter in this book is devoted to the legalities of social media communities; the *policies* your company will incorporate to protect its brand and its competitive marketplace position. This section focuses on social media guidelines, or the operating playbook that will be designed to both recruit employees and train them in ways they can maximize their social media activities for the benefit of your brand, customers, stakeholders, partners, prospects, and, of course, fellow coworkers.

For any business or organization, social media guidelines can empower employees by encouraging a critical mass of participation, which is essential for a successful social media marketing strategy. Conversely, strict social media guidelines can discourage people from leveraging one of the most important new communications tools for engaging with your customers. To be sure, businesses often struggle with seemingly contradictory issues when it comes to social media: they want to protect their brand while at the same time supporting the free expression of their employees. With properly constructed social media guidelines, there's no reason why you can't achieve both objectives. Surveys show that more than 70 percent of large companies and organizations have established social media guidelines as part of their overall corporate communications activities.[2] Eventually, as social media is woven into the marketing and sales fabric of every business, guidelines will be as common as the employee handbook or new hire orientation manual. Although policy and procedures documents will specify the dos and don'ts of using Twitter, Facebook, LinkedIn, Google+, YouTube, and other social media channels, your company "guidelines" will serve an equally important purpose by showing employees how they can help directly promote your business through company-hosted blogs and discussion forums, as well as through its social presence at company-managed LinkedIn groups, YouTube video channels, or business pages established on Facebook, LinkedIn, Google+, and other social platforms.

Why Are Social Media Guidelines Important?

More than likely your employees are already immersed in social media—some more than others—so there's a good chance their social sharing can and will spill over into the workplace. When e-mail was first introduced as the then-new major advancement in business communications in the early 1990s, company officials restricted e-mail accounts to selected employees, fearing unwanted disclosure of company information and corporate secrets. Similar alarms have been raised with social media and its inherent ease of information dissemination and exchange, especially with the virtually irrevocable nature of any content shared or posted in public forums and social networks. Companies that typically had been comfortable with traditional, highly controlled public relations and marketing communications functions now faced customers and stakeholders who expected businesses to operate with the new social era values of trans-parency, authenticity, immediacy, open dialogue, easy access, engagement, and trust. The truth is common sense rules of sharing company information didn't change when we transitioned from hand-delivered interoffice memos and "snail mail" to fax machines, and then later e-mail, text messaging, and social channels. Those same commonsense rules apply in the social world, and that's why you need to refresh your company's communications objectives in a formal social media guidelines document. Codifying your marketing prefer-ences, business style, and social sharing recommendations in your social media guidelines addresses two key business concerns: (1) senior management can sleep well knowing there is an official document detailing how employees should use social media channels on behalf of the company, and (2) employ-ees will be empowered with the necessary guidance and social networking parameters designed to position your company as a social networking leader.

What's more, your company needs social media guidelines because your business communications are no longer solely the function of your public rela-tions and marketing staff. Human resource representatives increasingly rely on social media to recruit and screen employee candidates. The ultimate low-cost focus group now may reside in various social forums and groups, where your product developers can share and exchange ideas with customers, partners, investors, and new business prospects. Social media has significantly altered the sales process, with leads generated via drilling down on enormous volumes of customer data, and product credibility is now built through online engage-ment. In addition, highly informed customers and prospects can accelerate buying cycles with information shared by your company, customers, stakehold-ers, and other interested parties. For customer service, social media has revo-lutionized opportunities to build greater customer satisfaction by offering new ways to deliver information and solve problems and issues, often in real time.

(continued)

(*continued*)

When it comes to social media, employees are an incredibly valuable asset that can be leveraged as brand ambassadors to amplify a company's marketing, sales, public relations, customer services, and human resources programs. Social media guidelines are essential and are extremely effective for formalizing the ways in which your employees can act as potent extensions and enhancements of your social media team; they also can provide direction regarding how to globally showcase your brand.

What Are Social Media Guidelines?

Social media guidelines are more than a set of operating procedures and advice for employees. Think of your guidelines as social enablers, or a means to stimulate, encourage, and support the active engagement of employees on behalf of your company as brand ambassadors. Chances are, most employees are so busy in their day-to-day routines that they are unaware of the full extent of your company's social media programs and how they can participate. The math is compelling. If your company has 100 employees, each with 500 followers on social networks, that translates into a potential marketing reach of 50,000 people. The fact that your company has elected to establish a formal set of guidelines is important recognition that it regards social media as a key strategic element of your company's marketing communications, as it should be.

Guidelines can stimulate company camaraderie, boost morale, and unify employees around shared business objectives. Viewed in that context, your social media guidelines should be designed to enhance your social media program by marshaling the collective potential of all employees with the common goal of reinforcing and expanding your company's marketing messaging in a wide array of public forums and social networks.

Social media guidelines thus can serve a two-fold purpose: they can inform all employees about the full extent of your social media outreach, and they can help secure contributions when you solicit employees to write for your company's internal or external blogs or need help broadcasting news, updates, and information to the extended audience available via a socially connected employee base. Published guidelines can effectively reinforce your company's commitment to social media and help *enroll* employees as active (and needed) participants.

Your social media guidelines can form a *cohesive strategy* for social engagement. Your employees will be advocates for your brand as well as serve as invaluable extensions of your customer service programs by offering various levels of support and feedback when they respond to online queries in social channels and engage in discussions or comments. It's not uncommon for customers and stakeholders to use Twitter, Facebook, and other social channels to sidestep traditional customer service tools such as call centers and e-mail by tweeting or posting status updates addressing problems, questions, or issues with a brand. A single social community manager or small team may not always be the first responder. Your guidelines provide employees with the confidence and skills needed to respond or engage in a manner consistent with your company's overall business communications strategy.

Social Media Guidelines Are a Reflection of Your Brand

When it comes to establishing your company's social media guidelines, perhaps the optimal strategy is to consider striking a balance between the need to protect and control a brand and the desire to leverage social media channels to widely market and promote your brand. You may have to choose what's practical, sensible, and, in certain circumstances, enforceable. And perhaps the last thing you want is for your social media guidelines to become a potential liability for your brand. During the Summer Olympics in 2012, the social media guidelines issued by the International Olympic Committee (IOC)[3] became the subject of news media stories and social media debate when spectators and even athletes complained that the guidelines were so restrictive that they stifled even the most modest of social media engagement.

For the international assemblage of athletes, the IOC put restrictions on tweets, prohibited live posts and comments during competition, banned video sharing from the Olympic village, restricted use of the Olympics logo, and even specified where and when the word *Olympic* could be used. On the unenforceable side, spectators could post photos to their heart's desire on any social media channel, but no videos. Olympic officials later backtracked from that spectator (i.e., customer) "guideline," explaining that the original intent was to prevent commercial entities from profiting from the international sporting event.[4]

By contract, SAS, a North Carolina–based business analytics and software firm with more than 13,000 employees worldwide, views social media in terms of customer value and new business development.[5] Its social media guidelines encourage employees to participate because it believes that additional company voices in the marketplace enhance the way it communicates the value of its products and services. The company acknowledges the merging of our personal and professional lives via social media and approaches the practical aspects of separating the personal from the professional by using different channels to speak to different audiences—but always mindful that anything posted online can be connected to company employment. Acknowledging that we live and work in a 24/7-connected world, SAS supports social media activities during working hours, when social engagement is tagged as part of an employee's job responsibilities.

(continued)

(continued)

How to Create Your Company's Social Media Guidelines

In constructing social media guidelines for your employees, clearly detail what's appropriate and what's not. Even though common sense should prevail most of the time, use examples to spell out what works best for your company. Detail the extent of your company's social media program and provide contact information should an employee have questions about posting comments, updates, videos, article links, photos, or tweets. Discuss what the social media team does on a day-to-day basis so that you can avoid duplicate postings in the same social channel. Your goal should be to coordinate and orchestrate your company's social media outreach. Your guidelines can go a long way in explaining the nuances of social media posting etiquette.

There is no reason to create your policies and guidelines in a vacuum. Before drafting your company's social media guidelines, consider holding meetings with individual or small groups of employees. Incorporate their questions, suggestions, concerns, and interests in the draft. Face-to-face meetings with employees will help gauge employee social experience levels and enable you to directly explain the objectives of employees serving as brand ambassadors for your company. Getting employee input before you publish the guidelines will reduce the need to issue revisions and updates, but do plan on regularly reviewing and updating the guidelines to account for changes in the social media landscape as well as new business strategies and objectives.

An ideal way to communicate changes is to use an internal blog that encourages employee comments and discussion. Notices regarding updated guidelines that are posted to the blog should be written in an informal, conversational style so that employees can better understand the thinking behind changes and recommendations. In building your company's guidelines, provide clear and unambiguous guidance on the right and wrong ways to use social media. Offer advice on the pros and cons of different social channels, focusing on social networks where employees can make the maximum impact for your company.

Your guidelines might be subject to legal review, especially if you cover areas of employee monitoring and recruiting. But be wary of attorneys erring on the side of litigation avoidance and turning your guidelines into a jumble of legalese guaranteed to stifle employee participation in social media. You are developing tips, recommendations, and guidance, not a policy document, which is covered in a separate section of this book.

Your social media guidelines can start as an extension of your existing company mission statement or summary of business objectives. Now add the social media component by discussing ways to leverage social engagement. Your social media guidelines should stress that there are three essential parts to promoting your brand in social media channels: how you show up, what you share, and how you share. *Showing up* refers to how you present yourself and your company. Every employee should review his or her social profile photos and bios to ensure there is an appropriate personal/business blend of information. Discuss how employees can use search via Google, LinkedIn, and other tools to maximize social engagement with customers and prospects. Your guidelines should discuss how employees can share *content of value* with their followers to stimulate discussions and ultimately drive traffic to your company's website. Corporate social media guidelines are widely published; use them as reference documents in the constructions of your company guidelines. Here are 10 recommendations you can incorporate into your guidelines to help employees maximize their business potential in social media channels:

1. Avoid *any* negative reference to competitors. If you wouldn't say it at a business event or social gathering, don't share it in a social media posting.
2. Social media engagement is about discussions, not the *direct* selling of products or services. Think about ways to stimulate interest in a topic, idea, or article that you read. If you share an article or blog post link, don't just drop in the link, tack on the words "Great article!" and leave. That's called a drive-by post, and in some social circles, it is viewed as spam. Explain why the article is important or what issues it raises or ask questions about it. Remember when you drive traffic to your post, you can deliver prospects to your brand.
3. Refrain from discussing products or services in development, pricing, or plans for mergers, acquisitions, or partnerships.
4. If you reference customers, do so carefully.
5. The exception to discussing products, services, and customers is mentioning or linking information published in company press releases, case studies, videos, recorded webinars, or other company-promoted marketing communications. Spread the good word, but watch out for duplicate posting in the same groups or social channels by fellow employees.
6. Be upfront and transparent concerning your company connection. Posting content on behalf of a company anonymously is generally not a fruitful strategy. Social media networkers like to engage with real people, not logos and avatars.

(continued)

(*continued*)

7. The secret to posting content in forums and discussion groups is the *indirect* marketing of a brand. Employees should leverage their *subject matter expertise* as a key sales and marketing strategy.
8. Customers and prospects may participate in the same forums, groups, and social networks. Be careful when posting the same content or links to multiple groups, forums, or business pages. Make every post count; change the messaging or theme of a post to match the unique interests or focus of each group, forum, or follower audience.
9. If you mention company product names and trademarks, make sure you check the official company style sheet for spelling and punctuation usage. Your brand does not want errors shared, reshared, reposted, and retweeted.
10. Monitor personal news, business updates, and career changes posted by your friends, followers, and connections. Change and news are ripe opportunities for personal and professional engagement.

Bottom-line recommendation: engage in social media channels as you would at a business meeting, industry event, or social gathering. It's all about how you show up and what you share.

Source: Joel Don[6] is principal of Comm Strategies,[7] a business communications consultancy that leverages public relations, reputation enhancement, and social media strategies to maximize business success. He also is social media community manager for the International Society of Automation.[8] Joel has worked for several public relations and marketing agencies and previously served as a public information officer at the University of California, Los Angeles, and the University of California, Irvine. He also directed business and financial communications at a Fortune 500 computer manufacturer.

Once you've created this type of internal culture and established your social media guidelines as suggested, it will be important to make sure everyone is kept abreast of the social media program. Your company may even use social networking tools for internal communications throughout the enterprise. Although you may believe the only people who really matter with social media are external constituents, the truth is that a strong internal communications team can play a huge role in the successful onboarding of a social media strategy. Fortunately, Maximize Social Business has as a contributor a thought leader in the field of internal communications and social media, Rachel Miller.

INTERNAL COMMUNICATIONS AND YOUR SOCIAL MEDIA STRATEGY: WHAT YOU NEED TO KNOW, BY RACHEL MILLER

The volume of information employees need to know when they join a company is vast. Does your communication checklist that notes health and safety procedures, organizational charts, and HR processes also include information about your company's social media strategy? It should.

Done well, the onboarding or induction phase is often conducted by a variety of employees, including HR managers, line managers, and peers. It is essential that your internal communication, either from one of these groups or from the communications team directly, educate and inform new hires about the social media strategy.

This is important because it equips them for success, letting them know from day one what is expected of them and what they can expect when it comes to social media use. This is not a one-way conversation. The company and its employees will have their own views and expectations when it comes to using social media. Have an open and transparent conversation upfront in order to avoid misunderstandings later.

This process shouldn't stop at the social media orientation phase. Make sure employees are aware of the boundaries and guidelines regarding social media and communicate them regularly. Having a fantastic strategy in place that isn't reviewed regularly means it can go out of date and lose relevancy. Best practice is to build in time to update, review, and refresh a social media strategy. Ensure that everyone understands it; what looks good on screen or paper needs to translate well with the workforce. Do employees know what the strategy means for them personally and professionally?

A role model recently emerged to provide guidance in this area. In the United Kingdom, the Local Government Association (LGA) has developed a Social Media Friendly Mark. It is a logo communications professionals can use internally to let employees know whether certain information is okay to be shared via social media. The guidance, images, and background are available publicly[9] for anyone to access. Initiatives such as this empower employees to make smart choices by clearly outlining what information can be shared (and therefore what can't).

An essential part of internal communicators' roles is finding ways to champion and integrate new channels and for employees to connect, collaborate, and communicate with the company. Create a communication culture of flexibility within boundaries by clearly outlining your strategy and inviting employees to have input.

(continued)

(*continued*)

Internal Communications versus External Communications

The lines between internal and external communication continue to blur, and social media plays a key part in this haziness. *Internal communication* is the term traditionally given to communication taking place inside an organization. However, it's not as black and white as that anymore.

The primary community for internal communication remains employees, but other external parties are often in the mix, too. This can include union officials, work councils, shareholders, investors, and future and former employees.

When viewed in the context of the broader communications team, internal communication is often deemed the same as or under the umbrella of corporate communication. Semantics aside, external communication takes place with customers and media, public and government affairs, corporate social responsibility, sponsorship, brand, events, and more.

Increasingly, we are seeing the divide between internal and external communications being shattered. Some communications agencies are merging their internal and external communications divisions to offer an integrated approach.

Rebecca Pain, business development manager at theblueballroom agency in the United Kingdom, which has taken this approach, says: "Information is in constant motion in today's digital world—what you say and do inside your business can directly affect your external reputation, and vice versa. We have removed the internal/external divide in recognition of the fact all audiences need to be considered, and combined internal communication and PR. This brings greater credibility, consistency and value to business communications as employees, customers, shareholders, partners and suppliers are all important stakeholders in business."[10]

It's always been the case that internal communication has the potential to be shared externally. It's brought into sharper focus due to the internal scrutiny that exists around social media, which makes it easier than ever for "internal" information to find its way to the outside world. My advice is to create and oversee internal communication with that in mind and ensure you have clear boundaries and guidelines in place.

People Who Matter

Time, money, and effort are spent creating effective external communication strategies and deciding how to engage with people who matter. The same should be true of internal communication. Your employees have the potential to be your best brand ambassadors.

The Games Makers from the London 2012 Olympics are an example. This merry troop of purple-uniformed, cheery, unpaid volunteers made my home city proud. They were pleasant, polite, helpful, knowledgeable, informative, passionate, dedicated, excited—the list of adjectives is endless.

The Institute of Internal Communication (IoIC) gave all 70,000 Games Makers a special award as *Communicators of the Year, 2012*, saying: "This is a group of people who took communication to the finishing line with style and expertise."

IoIC president Suzanne Peck says: "Never before has a group of disparate, diverse people come together so beautifully to form a cohesive and focused team that really made a difference. They excelled at communicating simply, clearly and cheerfully. Olympians, organizers and visitors heaped praise on how they made the Games sing, came to represent the spirit of the Olympics and helped create a show-stopping world extravaganza."[11]

Connecting the Dots

Many companies have persuaded executive teams to consider social media for use within an organization, but for many other internal communication professionals, the reality is that skeptical senior leaders and a workforce requesting social tools and access are at odds with each other.

Employees are more connected with technology than ever before and communicate collaboratively in their personal lives. However, when it comes to displaying the same traits professionally and people shift into professional mode, collaboration often stops. This may be for a variety of reasons, including organizational culture, technology limitations, geography, and the nature of roles.

The role of internal communication professionals is to connect the dots, influence stakeholders, and make smart choices that benefit employees and the company. Introduce social media the same way you would any other communications channel: with due care, attention, time, and resources. After all, social media is not something you do *to* employees, but *for* and *with* them.

Source: Rachel Miller[12] is an internal communications and social media strategist based in London, United Kingdom. Named *PR Week's* Top 29 under 29 professional communicators in the United Kingdom, she has worked in internal communications agency-side and in-house for global companies across the financial, automotive, health care, and railway sectors.[13]

Chapter 14   Managing the Risks

As companies begin to open their social media programs up to their employees, it's worth looking at what the potential risks are of implementing such a program and how to handle them. According to a 2012 study, only 24 percent of the Inc. 500 companies have a social media policy.[1] Those operating in heavily regulated industries should take extra precautions (which, unfortunately, go beyond the scope of this book), but be in touch with legal and compliance teams when creating and implementing the social media program. Nonetheless, there have been a number of debatable social media brand meltdowns, from the likes of Kenneth Cole,[2] Motrin,[3] American Red Cross,[4] McDonald's,[5] and others, and it's important for brands to consider how they should deal with crises that either begin on or bubble over to social media.

A number of additional glaring issues are emerging with the growth of social media in the workplace of which companies need to be mindful:

- **Social media content required for e-discovery:** Companies have always maintained archives of other documents, and now they're being required to provide social media content. For reference, one of the first cases of this was Gordon Partners et al. *v.* George S. Blumenthal et al.[6]

- **Increased requests for social media data during regulatory examinations:** One report indicates this was a growing trend starting in 2010 for financial services firms.[7] The same report also predicted that, "by the end of 2013, 50 percent of all companies will be asked to produce content from social media websites for eDiscovery."

- **Security risks:** Just as there are inherent online security risks when managing a website, digital properties require management and new solutions to help mitigate security risks.

- **Potential damaged brand reputation and loss of customer trust:** Some of the social media crises mentioned earlier in this chapter might be examples of this. More recent examples are cases involving Applebee's[8] and NASCAR.[9]

- **Lack of social media guidelines:** The lack of social media guidelines is a huge risk, because, without creating them as suggested in Chapter 13, employees in charge of implementing the strategy and company employees on a wider scale won't know how to professionally and properly represent the company brand.

Despite these risks, not having an updated and legally vetted social media policy might be the largest one. We are still at the potential tip of the iceberg of lawsuits involving companies and their employees regarding their use of social media, and if the PhoneDog LLC *v.* Kravitz[10] case that was tried in the California courts is any indication, there are still many reasons why companies (and employees) need to be vigilant.

In the case, a company (PhoneDog[11]) sued its former employee (Noah Kravitz[12]) for ownership of his Twitter account, which was originally under the name Phonedog_Noah and later renamed to his personal name under the agreement that he would also tweet on PhoneDog's behalf. When the two parted, in addition to Kravitz suing PhoneDog for revenue share breach of contract, PhoneDog countersued, asking for $340,000 according to the following calculation[13]:

$2.50 per follower × 17,000 followers × 8 months employed

A California court upheld the case,[14] but unfortunately for those looking for legal precedent, the case settled outside of court.[15] This is an excellent example of how lack of a social media policy can create bigger problems later, especially as an increased number of employees use social media in their personal lives as well as part of their jobs.

SOCIAL MEDIA POLICY

As opposed to a social media guidelines document created to raise the digital IQ of your employees as detailed in Chapter 13, the social media policy that I discussed in this chapter is meant to protect the employer from any potential damage done by an improper action taken by any employees on the company's, or their own, social media accounts. Just as employees may be required to sign nondisclosure agreements and other documents that dictate their rights and restrictions within the company, every company must have a similar policy signed by all of their employees vis-à-vis a social media policy.

Because I am not a lawyer and someone qualified from the legal profession should discuss all legal considerations for your business, I have called upon employment lawyer and social media and employment law contributor to Maximize Social Business, James Wu, to provide a legal perspective and further background on the creation and maintenance of a social media policy.

A BACKGROUND TO SOCIAL MEDIA POLICY CREATION,[16] BY JAMES WU

Creating a social media policy is a must-have for any company, but it can be hard to know what can be done lawfully and how to implement and maintain such a policy. Understanding that the law on social media policies constantly changes, let's consider where employers can start with this process.

What Can Employers Do, and How Do They Do It Lawfully?

Employers have a legitimate interest in making sure their employees are working during work time, being productive, and using company-provided computers and equipment for legitimate business purposes, including any social media–related activities. If an employee's job does not require access to Facebook, Twitter, Google+, LinkedIn, and other social media sites, some employers block access to these, along with many others, such as CNN and ESPN. The goal in doing so is to eliminate workplace web surfing. Some employers also deny workplace computer access to e-mail run through third parties like Gmail, Yahoo!, and Hotmail.

(continued)

(continued)

A greater number of employers, however, do not block such sites and e-mail services but rather maintain the option to monitor employees' computer, Internet, and telephone use. They do so lawfully because they tell their employees they should have no expectation of privacy. Generally, employers have a great deal of freedom in monitoring their employees if done for legitimate reasons and in as limited a way as to achieve these legitimate reasons. Employers should have policies that make clear in no uncertain terms that when an employee uses company-provided computers, Internet access, or other property, the employee consents to being monitored. These policies are generally found to be lawful, particularly when the employer owns the computers and equipment and/or the e-mail system and Internet access.[17] Furthermore, employees usually acknowledge their understanding of such policies by signing an acknowledgment form about the specific policy or an entire list of guidelines that includes such provisions. Whether an employer actually monitors all such activity is another question. The important takeaway here, however, is that if an employer promulgates properly drafted policies and notices, employees should not consider anything done using company-provided tools to be private.

Your Social Media Policy and Your Other Internal Policies

Once you've created a social media policy, it is not easy for a company to stay up to date regarding compliant workplace social media policy. Unfortunately, the law on social media use in the workplace changes so often that companies that want to have and maintain the best policies will likely need to update them fairly often. Also, once the company has a social media policy in place, it needs to ensure other workplace policies are also updated. That is, the social media policy cannot stand on its own. Social media is everywhere and affects everyone, and this omnipresence is a nightmare for employers because social media use intrudes upon some very divergent workplace issues. The following policies should be revised or implemented to ensure they coordinate with the social media policy:

- **Prohibited harassment/discrimination/retaliation policy:** Employers should update antiharassment and discrimination policies to reflect that an employee's online activities can rise to the level of prohibited harassment/discrimination. For example, when defining or describing prohibited harassment, your company's antiharassment policy should include examples such as posting sexually offensive material on social media sites, improperly using e-mail/text messaging, watching inappropriate content on a tablet while at work, or using derogatory or bullying language via social media.

- **Disciplinary/termination policy:** In most employee handbooks, employers typically list a variety of activities that exemplify behavior that may lead to "disciplinary action, up to and including termination." Update that list to include examples of improper use of social media, but remember that some activities, although disliked by an employer, cannot be prohibited. For example, in California, employers cannot prohibit employees from discussing wages.[18]

- **Confidential information/trade secret policy:** Employers often have policies and/or agreements prohibiting employees from revealing company trade secrets or confidential information. Update this policy to prohibit the use of computers, social media, and so on, in publishing such information. This revised policy should explicitly list what type of information the company considers to be protected confidential information or a trade secret.

- **Cell phone/driving policy:** Many states prohibit drivers from using cell phones while driving, but your company may want to take the most conservative approach to protect itself by prohibiting the use of cell phones for any purpose (except in emergency) while the employee is driving. This means no chatting on the phone, texting, or updating social media statuses while driving. If your state's law allows phone calls to be conducted hands-free (using an earphone, for example), employers should update such policies to comply with state laws.

- **Overtime work policy:** This policy is geared toward nonexempt employees (generally, those employees who are eligible for overtime).[19] Nonexempt employees who check e-mail and receive/respond to texts from their managers at night, update the company's blog at night, or otherwise work beyond 40 hours per week (and 8 hours per day in California) are entitled to overtime compensation for that work. An overtime work policy should state that employees can perform overtime work only when approved in advance. Employers should also make clear that employees can be disciplined for working overtime without advanced approval. Even if the company disciplines the employee for performing unapproved overtime, it should still pay for the overtime work to eliminate the risk of dealing with a wage and hour claim.

- **Complaint/open-door policy:** Most employees who choose to vent about their workplace, miniscule paycheck, or mean boss do so because they believe (often incorrectly) that doing so via Twitter or Facebook is a good way to vent to a small group of followers or friends. This, in turn, makes the employer look bad, among other things. To curb these online

(continued)

(*continued*)

rants, employers should consider providing stronger complaint/open-door policies. Encourage employees to resolve differences directly with coworkers, turn to the human resources department, go to a company ombudsperson, or call an anonymous toll-free line the company has set up for employee complaints. In addition to having such a policy, employers should foster a work environment that supports the policy by relying on and training good managers and supervisors to encourage open communication. By having a true open-door policy, employers may not only avoid having dirty laundry spread via social media[20] but may also be able to resolve many employee issues before they evolve into larger disputes and lawsuits.

These six policies are just a few that employers should keep in mind regarding the many issues social media creates in the workplace. There are others, including policies on workplace privacy, acceptable computer and equipment usage, and workplace violence that should also be considered.

Maintaining Your Social Media Policy

Just as the social media strategy is regularly maintained, it is equally important to update the social media policy because of the frequent evolution of rulings regarding social media. Focus on these three key areas:

1. Update the policies and/or handbook and resolve to stay updated at least once a year. Expect that some policies should be updated more frequently.
2. If an employer wants to take steps to discipline or terminate an employee as a result of something posted on social media, the employer should resolve to do so with great care. Employers need to maintain at-will employment relationships[21] when possible. Furthermore, employers never want to face lawsuits, so have termination decisions properly investigated and seek advice from an employment attorney.
3. Develop a solid relationship with an employment attorney (preferably someone in your company's state) before the company is sued. Retaining and paying a relatively minor fee to that attorney pales in comparison to the costs of litigating even one wrongful termination case.

James Y. Wu[22] has provided day-to-day counseling and advice to employers regarding compliance with employment laws and reducing the risks of employment-related claims and lawsuits for over 16 years. After practicing at some of the nation's leading law firms, James opened his own law office in order to continue to provide his top-notch service at a much more reasonable rate for his clients.[23] James earned his JD from Boston College Law School and both his BA and MA from Stanford University.

SOCIAL MEDIA AND CRISIS MANAGEMENT

Before implementing a social media strategy, many business leaders ask, "What happens if someone says something bad about our company in social media?" Social media has given the term *crisis communication* new meaning with its inherent ability for two-way communication. Long gone are the days when companies merely had official spokespeople provide the media a quote for the press to cover and potentially respond to, at most, a few of the public's questions. Now, any of the more than 1 billion social media users have the ability to directly ask a question to a brand via a digital outlet. For advice on how a company can handle the potentially risky and complex situation inherent with operating a social media presence, I asked Maximize Social Business contributor and expert on communications and online security Christopher Budd to weigh in.

CRISIS IN SOCIAL MEDIA, BY CHRISTOPHER BUDD

Social media has been a force for significant transformation in many areas of our lives. It enables us to stay in touch and share things quickly and easily with hundreds, if not thousands, of people. With social media, technology enhances and increases the impact and effect of humans' natural drive to create social bonds.

That last point is key to understanding social media: it hasn't created something new so much as it has increased the speed and potential amplification of what's already there. Social media hasn't created new ways for people to socialize: it makes their socializing easier, faster, and broader.

Understanding social media in this light is critical when we look at what happens when crisis hits the social media space. There's no other area where the technological leverage of social media has increased the impact and effect of people's natural desire to respond as when crisis hits social media. A crisis in social media for a business is like a crisis outside of social media—except that the crisis runs significantly faster and the damage is much greater. Thanks to social media, a crisis can truly destroy a business in a matter of days or even hours. And you don't need to have a presence on social media for this to happen. Crisis can overtake and harm your business even if you're not online. In fact, not being online puts you at even greater risk because it deprives you of important tools you can use to manage a crisis in the social media space.

(continued)

(continued)

What Is a Crisis in Social Media?

One of the things that is most challenging about crises in the social media space is that nearly anything can turn into a social media crisis if the right factors come together. Social media brings classic public relations and customer service together into a shared space, making it possible for them to feed off one another. A dissatisfied customer of 15 years ago privately working with a customer service person has been replaced by one voicing dissatisfaction in social media for everyone to see.

Perhaps the best example of this is the "United Breaks Guitars" song from 2009.[24] Canadian musician Dave Carroll wrote the song "United Breaks Guitars" and posted it to YouTube because he felt his concerns weren't being addressed after the air carrier broke his guitar, which he had checked. Within one day the video had received more than 150,000 views, ultimately forcing United Airlines to reach out to Carroll and try to rectify the situation in the public sphere. Although United Airlines did its best to manage the situation, the incident has become an Internet legend, permanently harming United Airlines' image to some degree.

What makes this situation a good example of the unpredictable way in which customer dissatisfaction can elevate to crisis level through social media amplification is the fact that at the outset of it, there was no way to predict that this particular negative customer service situation would turn into the social media crisis that it did. That's part of the challenge in this space and what makes defining a social media crisis so hard.

At a high level, you really can define a social media crisis much the same way that United States Supreme Court Justice Potter Stewart defined pornography: "I know it when I see it." Using more exact language, though, a social media crisis can be thought of as any situation that is occurring in social media spaces such as Twitter or Facebook that has risks of severely harming a company's reputation and that is out of control or on the verge of spiraling out of control. That last point is what is meant by the phrase "going viral": it means that the message or information, in this case a negative one, is being shared quickly and broadly through social media channels. This brings us back to the point about social media being leverage for people's natural socializing tendencies. It's natural for people to share negative or sensational news. In the past this would be done either in person or via the telephone, both of which impose certain limitations on how quickly information can be shared through social networks because of the one-to-one nature of the interaction. With social media and its one-to-many interactions, sharing happens at an exponential rate: in a few seconds a person can share information with hundreds or thousands of contacts, who then can do the same.

Understanding these essential qualities of a social media crisis is critical to understanding what to do to try to prevent them and what to do to manage them when they occur. Because social media crises are out-of-control negative situations in social media spaces that affect a company's reputation, your goal is to assert control in social media spaces as much as possible in an effort to effectively prevent and manage these situations.

An Ounce of Prevention

The film *War Games,* an early 1980s fount of wisdom, notes at the end, "A strange game. The only winning move is not to play." That certainly applies to handling social media crises. Hands down, the smartest thing you can do to handle social media crises is prevent them from starting in the first place.

Many social media crises start as a result of problems or issues in more traditional customer service or investor relations areas. Whether it's a problem with an unhappy customer, as in the "United Breaks Guitars" situation, or people unhappy with a company's philosophy or stance on an issue, you can often see social media crises start outside of social media and then move into that space. The catalyst that typically moves these situations to social media is a sense of frustration that concerns aren't being listened to in traditional channels. People often move their complaints into the more public social media sphere specifically to force a response that they believe they should get but aren't getting.

This means that your first area of focus in dealing with crises in social media is to work in those other areas as much as possible to keep frustration from reaching that tipping point. Good customer service—especially service that is mindful of the possibility of customers taking concerns to social media—can go a long way toward preventing social media crises by building a system for handling customer complaints that is aligned with this new reality.

In addition, maintaining a close tie between your social media team and customer service provides an extra layer of defense by making it possible for your social media team to quickly capture customer service complaints made in social media and direct them to direct, offline, one-on-one conversations with customer service. Some of the most effective social media brands now have special dedicated customer service staff to handle redirected social media requests. This is smart because a complaint in social media often has resulted from an inadequate customer service incident in the first place. And you can be sure that if a request for customer service help starts in a social

(continued)

(continued)

media space, any failure in handling it will be announced there. Like it or not, customer service needs that come through social media channels do need special handling.

These steps are meant to prevent social media crises from sparking in the first place—or if they do spark, these steps show you how to try to pour water on the situation before it can catch fire. One other thing that you should do to help prevent or minimize these situations is establish your presence online in a very measured and controlled way so that you can control and direct the discussion as much as possible. In practical terms this means establishing a clear and authoritative presence on Twitter and Facebook and then tailoring your presence to match the level of interactivity you can support. For example, if you do not have a strong dedicated social media team, consider limiting or disabling "inputs" like the Wall and Comments on Facebook to prevent your page from effectively being hijacked by others and used as a rally point against you. Also establishing and adhering to clear guidelines for acceptable postings can allow you to justify deleting obscene, hateful flame posts without being accused of censorship.

In Case of Emergency, Break Glass

Of course, as much as we may want to avoid any type of crisis through advance planning and caution, the fact is that nothing is guaranteed and events will confound our best planning. Even if you have the best customer service and maintain good control of your Facebook page, you may yet find yourself in the midst of a genuine social media crisis.

If that happens, what do you do?

To begin with, in the wise words of Douglas Adams in *The Hitchhiker's Guide to the Galaxy:* Don't panic! You'd be surprised just how wise that advice is in a crisis. Your first goal in managing a crisis is, to borrow from the Hippocratic Oath, to "First, do no harm." Many crises are made worse by poor handling; strive not to be part of that category.

Remember that an essential quality of a social media crisis is losing control of the situation. Panic on the part of those handling the situation quickly contributes to losing control.

Handling a social media crisis is very much like handling a public relations crisis and a customer service crisis combined—except that it's going to run a thousand times faster. Your goal is to establish control quickly and maintain control throughout. Successfully doing this can help prevent the situation from going viral.

You establish control quickly by responding to the issue at hand quickly, calmly, and reasonably and with honesty and candor. Once it moves into a social media sphere, treat what has happened in the past as a given; don't worry about changing it. If you are dealing with an irate customer who clearly has received inadequate service so far, acknowledge it as part of the process of resetting the dialogue. Honesty is always the best policy in crisis communications, and with social media, it's even more so.

As noted previously, where you can, try to take the dialogue offline to private channels. But don't make doing so a possible area of new contention. If the person resists at all, that's fine; just keep working toward a solution together.

Most social media crises have a core catalyst to them, so you want to focus your attention on that and not on the noise of those who pile on. How you address the core catalyst is what's going to make the situation go away or continue to drive it forward.

When the core catalyst is so broad that it involves too many people to engage with directly, you still want to focus on the core issue but adjust your tactics to be broader. For example, if you're addressing a social media crisis for a customer service situation that affects hundreds of people (like a planeload of people being locked on the tarmac for 9 hours), you want to respond to that broad core problem. A good example of an effective broad response like this was JetBlue's response to this sort of situation in 2011. JetBlue had its chief operating officer speak to the situation directly through a video blog.[25] His response was quick (within one day), calm, and reasonable, and he spoke with honesty and candor. It succeeded, too; the social media firestorm quickly evaporated after this was released.

Handling a social media crisis is actually not complicated. People with good common sense and a true sense of fair play and decency will know the right thing to do here naturally. So part of handling these situations is ensuring you have people like this on staff and have given them the means and support to do the right thing.

One of the greatest challenges in a social media crisis isn't responding correctly: it's keeping focused on solving the core catalyst. This is where keeping your channels to a manageable load helps because it keeps your staff from becoming overwhelmed. This is also where it's important for those responding to understand that not *every* post should be responded to, just those that are reasonable and related to the core problem. A social media crisis brings out people who have nothing else to do but post inflammatory comments. You're not going to win with them, so don't engage them. As the saying goes, "Don't feed the troll."

In crisis management online, a longer-term view applies. When the situation has passed, the points that are relevant to the core catalyst and

(continued)

(*continued*)

are reasonable are the ones that may do lasting harm to your brand. The Internet quickly forgets the myriad of "uR company sux" postings.

Conclusion

No one ever wants to go through a social media crisis of any size. They are incredibly intense affairs that, sadly, bring out the worst in people. The anonymity of the Internet gives many people the sense of having a license to say and do what they've wanted to for a long time but haven't felt able to. In the midst of these situations, understand that it's often not about you or your company at all: you're just the convenient whipping post for many people's frustrations.

This characteristic, though, means that once the situation has passed, the mob will forget and move on. And this is what you want to keep your eye on: the long-term situation. Keeping calm, addressing all points of reason, and being upfront will help you withstand the slings and arrows of the social media mob and get you to the place of final closure for the situation in as good shape as possible.

One final thing to understand: success in these situations is almost always measured in the negative. Don't focus on what happened as much as what didn't happen. Your response isn't a failure because you have a one-star Yelp review that's highly rated by others; your response is a success because that's all there is. There's no firestorm to follow on Twitter, no trending hashtag calling your company horrible, and no negative posts on Facebook. In the world of crisis management, and social media crisis management in particular, that mark of true success is when you take awful news and make it just bad.

Christopher Budd[26] works for Trend Micro, an Internet security company, and is an expert on communications, online security, and privacy. Christopher combines a former career as an Internet security engineer with his current career in communications to help people bridge the gap between the technical and communications realms and "make awful news just bad." Before Trend Micro, he worked as an independent communications consultant,[27] and prior to that, he was a 10-year veteran of the security response group at the Microsoft Corporation.

Chapter 15   Creating Your PDCA Workflow

Now that you've clarified who is going to do the work, how the strategy will be implemented in the company setting, and what potential risks lie ahead, it's time to create a workflow for implementing your social media strategy.

In Chapter 2, we discussed how the PDCA cycle or Deming cycle is a logical framework for planning, creating, implementing, and optimizing a social media strategy. However, after we've created the strategy and know who will implement it, we now need to better define and plan the D, or do, component.

The D component is basically a catalog or listing of all of the tactics that will be done daily, weekly, or monthly. These need to align with the social media strategy and be optimized over time. In addition to the D, other important considerations related to work management include creating a social media content calendar, developing a daily workflow, and constantly reviewing the workflow (the C [check] and A [action] steps in the PDCA cycle).

THE D

Most social media programs are very good at the *doing* part of social media, regardless of whether or not they have a social media strategy in place. But it's important to align your company's activities with its objectives, content strategy, and other elements involved with social media strategy creation.

The D includes actual activities you do on various social media channels considered important for your strategy. However, simply participating in social media in these channels is not enough; your actions must be aligned with all elements of your social media strategy, including content, frequency, engagement, influencer and brand outreach, and campaigns. As you can imagine, the D portion of your social media strategy has to be very structured in order to ensure your actions are aligned with the spirit, objective, and details built into your social media strategy so far.

In creating the D, it's important to understand on which platforms you'll be posting and at what frequency. This is obviously the most critical part of what you are doing, and if you already have a social media program, you probably have a number in mind. However, now you need to reevaluate and readjust what you've been doing with those elements based on your social media strategy so that everything is aligned moving forward.

The engagement piece, especially on the reactive side, is part of the D and may be limitless. Consider the limits on the D as being activities aligned with your social media strategy, whereas the reactive engagement is associated with the engagement strategy you'll have. Once you've created the D in as much detail as possible, it's time to create a social media content calendar.

CREATING YOUR SOCIAL MEDIA CALENDAR

All companies are media companies now. This is apparent through the convergence of communication and information as well as the importance of content. Despite what you might believe, your company is a media company just like any other newspaper or magazine out there. In fact, in some industries where the old media of newspapers and magazines have been slower to adapt to social media, your social media presence has the potential to become the most respected media for your field (this is especially true in some niche business-to-business industries). Harnessing the discipline that media companies have in consistency and creating relevant and high-quality content over time often sets the most successful companies apart in social media.

Now that you know what channels your company plans to use for sharing content, it's time to put that into a spreadsheet and create a schedule. Free social media content calendars and editorial calendar spreadsheets are available for download off the Internet.[1]

With a calendar, you can create a weekly or monthly publishing schedule that factors in on which channels you want to post, what types of content you'll want to share, and at what frequency you plan to publish. In a spreadsheet, prepopulate those areas where you need to share something at a predetermined time and on a specific channel. In this way your calendar will become completely filled, and you know what you'll be posting when and where.

If the D in your social media strategy aligns strategy with the tactics that you use every day, then the social media content calendar is your best friend. It will help you plan your D in a logical way and ensure the content you want to share is actually being shared.

However, your editorial calendar assists in more than simple organization. Once you determine what, where, and how often you'll be sharing, you can easily see where there are gaps in your content schedule. I personally like to color-code my social media content calendar. Use different colors to define the types of content you'll be sharing. For example, use one color for sharing your blog posts, one color for each one of your content bucket's curated content, another for occasional cross-promoting of social profiles, yet another for monthly campaigns, and so on.

When you put everything inside the editorial calendar, you can see where there are gaps in the publishing schedule. For those times, use curated content from relevant industry resources. Also consider cross-promoting your social media channels. For example, if there's a great conversation happening on one of your LinkedIn Groups, post a link to it on other social media channels. Are you joining a Twitter chat? Publicize it in other communities. Did you just start a new Google+ page? Spread the word elsewhere. Publicize your newsletter as well. Also consider sharing your new blog posts multiple times or even republishing older content that is still relevant.

This all might sound a bit overwhelming, but hopefully the use of a social media content calendar will prove to be a stress-free way to make sure you always have enough content across the various social media to post and that what is scheduled is in line with your social media strategy.

CREATING A DAILY WORKFLOW

When I speak about social media, I like to share a picture of an elephant standing on an inflatable ball. I use this paradigm because a lot of what I talk about in this book isn't necessarily rocket science. In fact, I would call social media part science, part art. I like to teach the science, but audience members have to be the artists for their own brands. And when it comes to day-to-day management of social media, it's a bit like that elephant balancing on the ball.

I recently signed up with a fitness club, and because I was focused on my goals, I signed up with a trainer to help me get back into shape. If you've ever done the same thing, you can probably relate to my experience.

The first time I met with my trainer, he told me to stand on one of those BOSU balls (the balls that look like they're cut in half). I was shaking trying to stay balanced, but after doing it for a few days in a row, I was able to stabilize and I wasn't shaking as much. By the end of the week, I could hold myself steady, but then my trainer came back and said, "I want you to do 20 squats while on the ball." I told him he was crazy but tried it anyway. The first few days with this task were brutal, but after a few days I was able to do that, too. This is because I was acquiring muscle memory. My body was learning and remembering how all my muscles needed to work in order to keep me steady on that ball and complete the exercise.

That's the elephant standing on the ball—and that is what happens when you start to implement your social media strategy. It becomes muscle memory. At first, it can seem overwhelming, but eventually you'll move through the routine because it's simply your daily workflow based on the D and the content calendar. By creating a daily workflow and sticking to it, you ensure you cover all the tasks in the D, are able to calculate the time spent, and can optimize your social media return on investment (ROI; discussed more in Chapter 17).

The elements of a daily workflow look similar to the circle we used with PDCA. Everything feeds off of and affects each other. On most days, you'll be doing one if not all five of these things.

Creating Content

This is the actual creation of content. These may include questions you want to ask as part of your engagement strategy, blog posts, photos you would embed in blog posts, photos uploaded to Instagram, or videos uploaded to YouTube. You need to create enough content on a regular basis that you can fulfill the requirements in your strategy-aligned social media content calendar.

Creating is the part of implementing the social media strategy that takes the most time. You won't necessarily constantly be engaging with audiences on social media platforms, and in those downtimes, you'll need to be creating content. Ideally, you have some amount of time set aside each day to create content, which may be inspired by an internal conversation, sparked by something you overheard, or developed from a social media conversation. You constantly need to think of new ideas and ways to create content for your company.

Curating Content

Curating falls into several different categories, including finding authoritative third-party content, gathering content from fans, and sharing conversations you have with fans. Curating also takes time, especially if you're trying to fill needs for specific types of content buckets, but it is something you need to have ready on a regular basis. The newer the content is, the more relevant and effective it is. This means it needs to be done regularly throughout your week so that you can share it daily.

One thing that can help with curation is taking the time to do it every morning. What are people in your industry reading for their news in the morning? What sort of response did you get from your community in the last day? By looking for curation fodder early in the day, you'll find a wealth of content to share over the course of that day. This also creates a nice buffer of content to fill in any upcoming gaps in the social media editorial calendar.

Sharing

Sharing overlaps with the notion of curating, but this is the actual action of posting all the content you created and curated according to the social media content calendar. Several posting tools are available to make sharing throughout the day easier, but even with these tools, it takes time to post content when you have a robust social media calendar. You'll also want to make sure you properly use targeting features in Facebook pages and LinkedIn company page status updates for each post as well as ensure the timing and hashtag optimization for each post for optimal sharing.

Engaging

Engaging has two parts: proactive engagement and reactive engagement. As noted earlier in this chapter, there's no limit to the amount of reactive engagement you'll receive as your brand becomes more popular on social media. Proactive engagement, on the other hand, should be done whenever you can, whether it is with your brand ambassadors, through influencer outreach, or by looking at the timeline of your followers and recognizing content from people you haven't been in touch with for a while. For instance, if you have Twitter lists or Google+ circles, you can easily find different segments of your audience and social media users regularly to engage with.

Obviously, social media is a two-way conversation. If you're talking about only your company or your industry, your influence is going to be limited. It's when you actually proactively start to talk to other people in social media (that is, average social media users) that people become fans of your company. People see conversations taking place and notice that your brand actually has a personality. When your company starts sharing the conversations or photos and videos of other social media users, your engagement rises to a new level.

The other part of engaging should be aligned with brand ambassador and influencer outreach strategies. Depending on the month or the timing of these specific outreach campaigns, this may be where a lot of your engagement time is best spent.

I find that *engagement* is one of the most talked about yet least understood terms in social media marketing. Engaging with social media users on a personal level can take many forms, but I find the following case study by Jason Eng from Sony Electronics to be an excellent example of how you can easily engage with your customers as part of your social media strategy.

SOCIAL MEDIA ENGAGEMENT: FOCUS ON BUILDING RELATIONSHIPS, BY JASON ENG

Over a year ago there was a promise to deliver firmware updates for two camera models on specific dates. We had put these dates on our website, and because these updates were for popular camera models, our fans were eagerly waiting for those dates to come. Unfortunately, we later learned that the firmware updates were still being tested, which was in the best interest of the users and but meant that they could not be released on the promised dates. Instead of waiting for the promised dates to come and go, I proactively started to reach out to users who had shown interest in these updates on social media. I simply apologized for the delay of the firmware updates and explained that they were still being tested and quality checked. I apologized for the inconvenience but also thanked them for their continued support. The reactions were as expected. People were frustrated and disappointed because we had promised something on a date and could not deliver. But they were also forgiving, understanding that it *was* in their best interest that we deliver an update that was stable. They also were appreciative of the proactive action we took to inform them of the delay, instead of waiting to react to users complaining. In addition, we received compliments from our followers on Twitter regarding our response time. We were able to turn a negative into a positive.

We have since been doing our best to use our social avenues to engage. We promote our products and inform followers on social media about our programs and promotions. But we also share user-generated content and engage in conversation with users, which has helped us build a steady following that quadrupled in size in one year. Our fans have been more than willing to help promote our social networks as we have continued to engage with them consistently. We have also seen a positive impact of personal interaction on social media from our employee social efforts with our product users. I was personally told by someone that he purchased a camera based on my recommendation, something that would not have happened had I not taken the time to engage personally with the user. From a social media perspective, the focus has been on the social relationships and it has turned out to be very positive.

Jason Eng[2] is a senior social media strategist and community manager at Sony Electronics Professional Solutions of America.[3]

Experimenting

This is an important part of your social media workflow because social media is a never-ending experiment. Traditional social media campaigns fall under this category, but you should always be experimenting and finding new ways to engage with your following, whether it's experimenting with sharing content on new platforms or developing new categories of content that aren't part of your content buckets. You constantly need to shake things up in order to find ways to make your social media strategy more engaging and efficient.

A daily workflow is supported by the strategy, the D tactics, and the social media content calendar. The remaining parts of the PDCA that warrant discussion are the C and the A.

REVIEWING YOUR WORKFLOW: THE C AND THEN A

The C involves taking the metrics and reviewing them regularly. (Chapter 17 provides information on the types of metrics you can include in the social media strategy.) The A requires reviewing the PDCA workflow and optimizing it based on insight gleaned from these metrics. The daily workflow and editorial calendar should constantly be optimized accordingly.

The C step includes a regular review on a weekly, monthly, or quarterly basis. I believe that certain trends take awhile to show results, so in terms of optimizing the content calendar, the D, or work tactics, it may be best to review things quarterly. Regardless of how often you do it, it is valuable to step back and optimize those different content buckets, your sharing frequency, and the platforms on which you share content.

By reviewing your workflow, you may find you're spending an incredible amount of time curating when you're actually getting the best engagement from your own content. Or perhaps engagement is taking a lot of time each day, and you haven't been able to write better-quality blog posts. In that case you may need to spend less time on engagement and more time on the creation. The answers will lie in the data and how they correlate with your D.

Every single company differs, and it's only by regularly reviewing and optimizing according to the A part of the PDCA cycle that you're able to increase the effectiveness and ROI of the social media program based on your company's definition of success.

Your PDCA workflow, creation of a social media content calendar, and catalog and optimization of tactics, as well as workflow over time, form the heart of an optimized social media strategy. They help guarantee the best efforts of increasing your ROI over time.

Sticking to the strict guidelines outlined in your strategy, as well as those noted on the social media content calendar, is not easy for any organization. But as it's been said, "If content is king, consistency is queen." Consistency in social media and sticking to a plan are critical components in determining how successful the implementation of a social media strategy is.

Chapter 16   Integrating Your Social Media Strategy

Early in this book, you conducted a social media audit in order to look at all of your digital marketing properties for the purpose of integrating them into your social media strategy. Now it's time to make this integration a cohesive part of the social media strategy.

Integrating social with other digital marketing properties requires more than simply ensuring a social media program does not exist as a silo within your marketing organization. Maximize Social Business is fortunate to have a contributor, Joseph Ruiz, who specializes in social media marketing integration and helps companies through the digital convergence of SoLoMo (Social Local Mobile). Joseph can shed further background on the importance of this subject and benefits of integration.

A BACKGROUND ON INTEGRATING SOCIAL WITH YOUR OTHER DIGITAL MARKETING PROPERTIES, BY JOSEPH RUIZ

Integrating social media with other digital marketing properties is critical for many reasons, the first being that consumers are increasingly social.

Consumers are social.

- Consumers are empowered by technology and the Internet: 1.7 billion people around the world will access the Internet using a mobile device in 2013. By 2016 this number is expected to grow to 2.5 billion.[1]

Consumers are mobile.

- Mobile search has grown 500 percent in the past two years (2010 and 2011).[2]
- Mobile search is always on. Seventy-seven percent of mobile searches occur in the home or office.
- Mobile search generates almost two follow-up actions.[3]

Consumers are local.

- Forty-three percent of total Google searches are local.[4]

Consumers increasingly use multiple channels.

- Mobile search drives multichannel conversations.
- Seventy-three percent of mobile search drives additional action and behaviors such as sharing, visiting locations, doing continued research, and making purchases.[5]

Reaching social consumers requires an integrated marketing approach that delivers a seamless customer experience. This approach requires a different mindset, one that recognizes that reaching these consumers requires collaboration and open communication internally and externally. Marketing assets must be aligned to attract and retain this new breed of consumer.

Benefits of Integrating Social into Your Marketing

- **Social is an opportunity to have a voice and listen**. It allows organizations to actively engage customers and partners by listening, asking, observing, and adapting.
- **Social is a venue to let your organization's personality shine**. People want to do business with people, not be inundated with advertising.
- **Social enables organizations to identify and solve problems and be responsive**. Social businesses are also able to adapt to the communications preferences of constituents and offer feedback right as conversations are happening. A social organization has the ability to hear from all stakeholders, internal and external.

- **Social influence is greatly expanded in an organization with a healthy social culture**. Customers share experiences with others and create word-of-mouth opportunities. Pepsico's Employee Program[6] is a great example of how the company's corporate culture offers chances for colleagues to share news and information about company products and services. Strive to be a company that has employees so delighted they'll naturally want to amplify their satisfaction socially.
- **Social is connection**. Most organizations are aligned by function, and although this is often necessary, it can create connection barriers or silos. Silos occur because employees tend to focus on their particular tasks or operations and fail to see the larger customer experience objectives. Traditionally, marketing efforts are focused externally with little internal communication.

  Organizations that add social to the marketing mix develop a different mindset, recognizing that a differentiating customer experience requires internal alignment of values. Leaders work to ensure that collaboration and engagement across all touch points results in productive conversations by tapping into the collective experience of all colleagues.
- **Social allows customers and prospects to interact with the brand in more personal ways**. Consumers want to share successes and be understood. Social companies with Facebook pages, for example, offer a venue where a brand can hear directly from the consumer without a face-to-face meeting or a formal notice.

A New Socially Integrated Mindset

Infusing social into a business doesn't mean that a company has to abandon tried-and-true marketing tactics. Being a social business requires a different mindset; it updates effective traditional marketing practices by maximizing appropriate calls to action and website references and carefully and thoughtfully positions opportunities for feedback across the marketing mix.[7]

Two-way communications is a must in the social media realm; the consumer's voice must be heard, and, if not, it may encourage potential consumers to move along to a merchant who responds rapidly. Buyers expect brands to dole out tailored offers and solutions to meet consumer demands. They also expect a consistent experience.

Based on the Economic Intelligence Unit (EIU) survey of retailers about what they need to build a successful social media strategy, the *Economist* reports that success requires the following four Cs for shopper success[8]:

1. **Consistency:** The brand promise should remain consistent across all channels, including social media.

(continued)

(*continued*)

2. **Community:** In contrast to the idea that the retailer should always be in control of the message, social media is the turf of the community of individuals who share an interest in a brand or product.
3. **Collaboration:** Only when insights are shared effectively across departments will social media deliver optimal value.
4. **Commitment:** At all levels of an organization, buy in to social media needs to be cultivated, supported, and mutually sustained to realize the benefits.

Achieving social success requires a different management style, one that relinquishes control and embraces the principles of:

• Participation, to ensure open dialogue.
• Purpose, which is the ability to identify progress toward overall goals and objectives.
• Performance, which advocates community-based ideas corporately.

Social Empowers Customers/Prospects and (Just as Importantly) Colleagues

Social networking adds relational power to your existing marketing. It enables unprecedented connectivity with the consumer, providing marketers with the ability to truly enhance consumers' lives. Social networking allows marketers to make marketing memorable. There are an unlimited number of ways to creatively integrate social into campaigns to make them exciting for marketers and consumers alike. People are interactive and love to share their voices and take part in games and promotions that generate buzz.

Just as customers are empowered with knowledge through their personal networks, social businesses keep colleagues informed and openly communicate with employees by:

• Communicating company initiatives.
• Listening to feedback and input.
• Mapping consumer touch points (whether through e-mail, in stores, on a social platform, or at a customer service center).
• Encouraging sharing and collaboration across functions, especially those who have ongoing contact with customers/prospects.

A healthy social business will inherently energize existing marketing efforts through empowered employees.

Source: Joseph Ruiz[9] is president of Strategic Marketing Solutions,[10] a full-service marketing and consulting firm specializing in web-based integrated relationship marketing. Joe thrives on the ever-changing nature of marketing in the digital age, embracing interactive opportunities while applying three decades of hands-on expertise in online and traditional marketing.

EXTENDING YOUR SOCIAL MEDIA STRATEGY TO YOUR EXISTING MARKETING CHANNELS

In light of Joseph Ruiz's advice, it's time to turn back to the social media audit and see what action items we need to extend beyond our existing marketing channels. These items are a bare minimum of what is possible, so use this as the starting point to maximize your social presence.

Website

Social media should not sit in a silo, and because some of the main objectives of this social media strategic plan are to both engage customers where they are as well as extend your brand into social media communities, it is recommended that at a minimum the following areas of your website, regardless of social media strategy objective, be integrated with your social media activities:

- All of your social properties should be represented with an icon on every page so that social media users who visit your website will see your affiliations and potentially "soft convert" by joining one of your social communities, even if they don't invoke any action on your website. If you are trying to drive brand awareness for newer channels, prominently feature the social media icons above the fold of each page.
- Google+ and Facebook have social widgets that allow you to show faces of people who have already liked/circled your business/fan page. It cannot be overstated how important potentially seeing photos of friends who have already liked your brand is. This may entice visitors to do the same. These face boxes should be used on every page, perhaps on the bottom or side banner as a contrast to the social icons on the top of each page.
- For search engine optimization (SEO) purposes, Google+ and Facebook also allow you to +1/like your website URL outside of your presence in these communities. It is suggested that these buttons appear on your website as well.
- Your blog should be implemented in a way that there is seamless navigation between blog content and other content. In other words, given your social presence and the SEO benefits of having a blog, more and more visitors will land on your blog page instead of your legacy

content pages; therefore, you need to make it easy for them to move from the blog to other pages on your website.

- Each blog post should have social share buttons. There are many ways to implement this, but consider displaying them at the top of each post and in a way that shows the number of people who have shared. These numbers—once your social share numbers increase—give instant credibility to your content. Note that you should include social share buttons only for strategic channels as defined by your specific social media strategy plan.

Newsletter

Your company is probably engaging in some type of e-mail marketing, and perhaps it has a variety of newsletters that are segmented for different demographic groups in your database. The following should be done to integrate your social media presence with your newsletters by ensuring they include any or all of the following types of social content:

- Announcement of new social media campaigns or events
- Content shared in social media, both popular blog posts as well as noted third-party content
  - o These can be shared to provide more of a resource to readers, encourage them to keep their subscriptions, and look forward to future newsletters.
- Interesting discussions happening in social media channels
  - o You can encourage your readers to chime in on the conversation and thereby increase your membership.
- Links to your social media accounts
  - o These should be featured in your newsletter to allow those who weren't aware of your brand's social media presence to easily become fans.

Pay-per-Click Advertising

This section will be relevant if your company is already implementing pay-per-click (PPC) campaigns to encourage Internet visitors using search engines to visit your company's website for various relevant keywords. Earlier chapters recommended investigating whether social PPC ads provided by Facebook, Twitter, and LinkedIn to build awareness and reach a greater number of social media users was a worthwhile investment for your company. If there is no budget for social ads, consider allocating part of a PPC budget to these social ads. Start with a 10 percent share for social media until the campaign goals are met. Of course, social PPC ads do not need to stop once fan/follower goals are reached; they can continue to be used to drive social media users to specific apps or posts concerning social media campaigns, as well as landing pages.

Integrate Your Data

Given the trend of big social data, it's time to consider how you can actually integrate this information throughout the organization. However, considering how much big social data exists, this is not a trivial task:

- Facebook processes 2.5 billion pieces of content and ingests 500+ terabytes of data a day.[11]
- Twitter processes 400 million tweets a day.[12]
- Instagram users upload 40 million photos per day.[13]
- The Google +1 button is used 5 billion times a day.[14]
- Seventy-two hours of video are uploaded to YouTube every minute.[15]

We are not interested in sheer numbers, however, but in what company objectives we can further by applying these data. Two primary areas where marketers can leverage social big data include:

- **Consumer insights:** What are consumers saying about you and your competitors? What adjectives or adverbs do they use to describe your products and services? Is the sentiment analysis of their public conversations positive or negative? How do all of these insights change over time? Leveraging social big data internally gives companies unparalleled access to understanding how your company is truly being discussed in public.
- **Market research:** Early in my career, I interviewed for a brand manager position in the product marketing division of a global consumer packaged goods company. What I learned then (before the emergence of

social media) was that brands spent a lot of money on user focus groups to determine the market for their products and ensure that features welcomed by their target would be included in the final product. Leveraging social big data allows you to do similar market research 24/7. Although it isn't free to do this because of the investment required to buy the right social listening tools and analyze the data, it could be a cost-effective alternative if you want to gather general public market research data.

From a market research perspective, social big data can help:

- Provide an infinite source of data regarding consumer demographics and buying trends.
- Gauge consumer interests and how they interact with competitors and content.
- Measure aggregate interaction between a brand and the public.

From a marketing perspective, leveraging big social data can help provide targeted products and promotions to targeted demographics.

If this sound too good to be true, consider the following list of case studies that illustrate the importance that big social data might have for your business:

- A Pamplin College of Business study confirmed that the existence of safety and performance defects in automobiles is strongly predicted by the incidence of automotive reports in social media.[16]
- Next Big Sound predicts record sales from social media conversations—and record companies buy their analysis.[17]
- WiseWindow provides real-time social data analysis to financial investors, the result increasing investment returns by more than 30 percent annually.[18]
- T-Mobile analysis of customer data and social media information cut customer defections in half in one quarter.[19]

The Big Social Data Challenge

Data integration is nothing new for marketers, but social big data integration might be a by-product of your social media strategy that can help your organization in many unpredictable ways. The following benefits of integration revealed by the IBM Institute for Business Value Global CMO Study found that chief marketing officers (CMOs) in outperforming organizations invest more effort in integrating and using data to foster customer relationships for the following purposes[20]:

- Segmentation/targeting (67 percent)
- Presales product education (56 percent)
- Needs-based content (54 percent)
- Delivering offers to buy (58 percent)

In addition, one survey reported that 65 percent of businesses in 2012 already believed that analyzing and gleaning insight from large data sets from social interaction happening in real time was important or very important to their business.[21] This can be achieved through use of social customer relationship management (CRM), one platform that can be used to leverage data sets and apply them to better managing customers and prospects.

There is some confusion regarding what, specifically, social CRM is. One of the thought leaders in the field, Paul Greenberg, defines it as follows[22]:

> Social CRM is a philosophy and a business strategy, supported by a technology platform, business rules, workflow, processes and social characteristics, designed to engage the customer in a collaborative conversation in order to provide mutually beneficial value in a trusted and transparent business environment. It's the company's response to the customer's ownership of the conversation.

Having a sales background, I like to take a slightly different yet targeted approach by applying a social layer to traditional CRM platforms like Salesforce.com and sharing that data internally. Very simply, if we can add social big data, segmented by user, into our CRM systems and then share that data between sales, marketing, customer support, and product development, we are able to leverage social data enterprise-wide for whatever business purpose we have.

In other words, by leveraging social big data in a targeted way using social CRM tools and sharing those data internally, it can help the social media strategy become implemented enterprise-wide. The problem is that leveraging social big data at this level requires both the implementation of robust tools and a company that has already evolved from using social media strategically in its marketing and communications to one that is already a social business. This is the reason why a recent study found that only 16 percent of companies surveyed had adopted a true social CRM platform.[23]

A step-by-step guide to leveraging social big data goes beyond the scope of this book, but you should be aware of the potential for integrating social far beyond current marketing properties. By creating the right organization, investing in the right tools, and always looking for better ways to integrate social data internally, you will undoubtedly be able to maximize your social in unexpected ways well into the future.

Chapter 17   The ROI of Your Social Media Strategy

Previous chapters in this book illustrated the depth and breadth of social media and what can be included in a strategy, depending on the specific objectives of your company. However, before you commit to everything, it is important to consider what the costs and return on investment (ROI) mean for your company.

Although some companies are still confused about the ROI of social media, they realize the need to incorporate it into an existing communications channel simply because so many people are using it. Based on my experience, I've noticed there's usually a three-stage approach to adopting social media within a company culture.

First, companies usually ask why they need to use social media. Statistics reveal that more than 90 percent of businesses with 100 or more employees are already using social media in their marketing mix,[1] and those that don't are definitely in the minority. Even if a company has limited social media that can't expand, there is often a concern about risk (which I hope I helped you mitigate) and whether social media actually has an ROI. My goal with this chapter is to illustrate why it is important, how to achieve optimal performance, and how to execute properly so that you can then educate and convince people within your company of the same.

Companies then begin to think maybe they should consider using social media. They start on a few channels to test the space. They may have limited resources, but undoubtedly, sometimes without even having robust metrics, they intuitively see the need and results. This leads to the third stage, when companies ask how they can do more with social media. Once companies reach this third stage, there is no turning back.

Companies in the third stage already understand that adding a social layer to their business is part of their corporate infrastructure. Proving your social media program's ROI, then, is much more important at those companies in the earlier stages of social media adoption. With this in mind, let's return back to look at how the social media strategy you created using this book can help you determine and optimize the ROI of your social media program.

SOCIAL AS PART OF YOUR CORPORATE INFRASTRUCTURE

Gary Vaynerchuk, noted social media guru and author of *Crush It* and *The Thank You Economy*, was being hounded in a boardroom and repeatedly asked, "What is the ROI of social media?" He responded, "What's the ROI of your mother?"[2] Gary is known to be a passionate keynote speaker in the social media world, and I didn't originally like that quote, as I thought it ignored the question without properly addressing it. I tweeted to Gary that I thought his comment wasn't really driving home the message that there is ROI in social media. His response was, "It creates context to the conversation, have u asked what the ROI of outdoor media or print or TV or Radio is lately . . . that is where it gets interesting."[3] He is absolutely correct.

As you start incorporating social media into your company with your social media strategy, it begins enveloping the entire enterprise and therefore has the potential to increase profits and sales, decrease expenses, and increase brand equity, among many other intangible benefits.

Once you perceive social as part of the company infrastructure, that question about ROI never goes away. The challenge is then understanding the metrics and achieving proper performance in order to facilitate resource needs so that the greatest ROI is achieved.

SOCIAL MEDIA METRICS TO SUPPORT THE OBJECTIVE

Early in this book I emphasized the importance of establishing a business objective for your social media strategy. To determine whether that objective was met, use the PDCA framework and check the results of your social media strategy. The metrics that matter in calculating the effectiveness of a strategy show whether you achieved your objective or not through social media efforts. Many make the mistake of using the social media metrics provided by their social media dashboards or other analytical applications, which may not be the most important figures to use when assessing the success of a social media strategy in meeting your specific objectives. Platforms such as Sprout Social and HootSuite, as well as special analytics applications such as Crowdbooster, SocialBro, Twitter Counter, and TweetReach, provide an array of metrics that may or may not be useful, and you can easily be bombarded by an overload of social media metrics that may be totally irrelevant to what you want to achieve with your social media strategy.

Before discussing what metrics you need to support your objectives, it's important to understand you should already have metrics in place for your current digital activities. These metrics should include:

- Cost per impression
- Value of a website visitor
- Cost of a website visitor
- Lifetime value of a customer (CLV)
- Cost of acquisition of a new customer
- Cost to retain a new customer

Having these baseline metrics will help you calculate the ROI of your social media strategy by applying these metrics to those website visitors' conversions referred from social media or your blog, as well as customers acquired directly through the efforts of implementing the social media strategy.

There are primarily three types of metrics I like to consider in evaluating the ROI of a social media strategy:

- **Primary metrics**, which directly affect your strategic goals and tie your social media efforts and business objectives together
- **Secondary metrics**, which indirectly affect your strategic goals and look only at the effectiveness of your social media strategy
- **Comparative metrics**, which show how well you compare to your competition and help in establishing baselines

All these metrics are important in analyzing and optimizing a social media program. Ultimately, ROI is tied to metrics, which show how social media contributed to overall objectives. Your reporting may not provide the information needed to calculate the ROI. If you don't have the proper internal infrastructure to calculate ROI, reporting on the proper metrics may be impossible.

Primary Metrics

Primary metrics look directly at how social media affected your reaching (or failing to reach) the objectives in your social media strategy. If one of the objectives was to increase sales through the use of social media, you can calculate how many leads, conversions, and sales you made through social media channels and compare this against the total cost of bringing in this revenue. As another metric, you could examine repeat business by comparing repeating customers with new customers. If you download customer data through a social customer relationship management tool and look at all the touch points, you may be able to determine how many customers engaged with your company through social media and how they affected sales. Did they buy more or less than customers who didn't use social media? Your ability to measure all of these depends on whether or not you have the right tracking system(s) in place to capture these data.

Secondary Metrics

Secondary metrics show only the effectiveness of your social media program and don't necessarily tie into your social media objective. They're simple to calculate and easily accessible through your social media dashboard, and they can be utilized to help improve the efficiency of your tactics in social media.

You should consider several potential secondary metrics found on social media dashboards and through analytics applications, both free and paid:

- Social reach (total number of social media followers)
- Social views (total number of page views on Facebook, LinkedIn, YouTube, etc.)
- Social mentions (number of times you were mentioned)
- Social conversations (number of conversations you had)
- Social-referred website traffic (amount, quality, conversions, etc.)
- Social content views (such as on YouTube)
- Engagement (likes, comments)
- Amplification (retweets, shares)
- Impressions (how many impressions your content receives in news feeds)
- Social clicks (what content is clicked on what sites)
- Sentiment
- Influence
- Search volume
- Inbound links

Comparative Metrics

Most companies already compare themselves to competitors in many different ways, so adding social media to the mix adds an extra layer. This is where the third metric—comparative metrics—comes into play. When comparing your company to an industry role model, these can provide baseline metrics for improvement, especially if your company is late in implementing a social program on a certain channel. These comparative metrics could include:

- Social share of voice
- Social reach
- Social mentions

- Engagement
- Social sentiment
- Influence

Ultimately, there is no single cookie-cutter approach to tying all these metrics to a specific strategy. You need to decide which to use based on your strategy, but once you've done that, these metrics can help calculate the ROI, effectiveness, and competitiveness of your social media program.

REVIEWING YOUR PDCA WORKFLOW

With the exception of the cost of social media tools in which your company may or may not invest, we know social media is not free because it requires time and resources to properly implement it. When examining expenses related to your social media strategy to judge how much your social media investment is, it's important to consider what the brunt of those expenses will be. Ultimately, that expense relates to the D in your PDCA workflow. And noted in Chapter 15 about creating a daily workflow, the following elements will be included:

- Creating content
- Curating content
- Sharing
- Engaging
- Experimenting

By adjusting how much time and effort is invested in each of these daily workflow elements, including those programs that have a large time investment, you can adjust to strive for more efficiency and a higher ROI.

Some things in the daily workflow, such as reactive engagement, cannot be eliminated. The reality of social media is that the more you engage, the more reactive engagement you receive. Once you receive it, you can't simply ignore a conversation. You also can't predict the volume of social conversations you'll receive. If you become popular and a lot of people are saying a lot of things about you, you can expect the amount of time you spend on reactive engagement to increase.

However, content creation and the amount of time spent curating, sharing, and proactively engaging will vary and can be adjusted regularly to aid your social strategy ROI. By looking at your metrics regularly, you'll be able to tell which platforms deserve more or less of your attention and which D tactics are more effective than others. Optimizing and tweaking these tasks can help achieve greater efficiency for maximized ROI.

MAXIMIZING YOUR SOCIAL ROI

Maximizing your social ROI obviously has two components: the return that is received and the investment put forth. Based on the social media strategy and metrics created, the first thing to calculate is whether there is a positive or negative ROI. You also need to compare your actual outcome with the projected outcome, as discussed in Chapter 3. If we have positive ROI (and I hope you do!), there are only two things you can do: (1) invest in greater social media resources and ramp up a phased approach you may have taken or (2) increase the frequency and/or content in which you are implementing social media. If you have a positive social media ROI, you can also broaden the social media scope. In addition to the increase in content, frequency, and engagement, perhaps you want to consider reaching out to more brand advocates and influencers. Maybe it's time to launch on a platform that wasn't originally included in the social media strategy. When you achieve that positive ROI in social media, you're at that final stage of adoption, which involves asking what more your company can do. And as illustrated by this book, there are many more things your company could be doing. Hopefully, the advice in this book will help you raise and scale your ROI as much as possible.

What if you experience a negative ROI? Negative ROI happens when either your expectations were too high or for some reason things didn't go according to plan. This happens all the time. Before you pull the plug or tear up your social media strategy (or complain to the author of this book), ask yourself these four questions to see what can be optimized to turn that negative ROI metric into a positive one.

- **Are your activities aligned with your social strategy?** It's very easy to veer off the social strategy if you aren't diligent in the implementation of your social media program. Perhaps the person running your social media program wasn't educated enough on all of the platforms or did not have enough knowledge on how to best implement the strategy. Take the time to conduct an audit to see whether you implemented according to plan.

- **Has your social strategy been implemented properly?** Perhaps you knew what you wanted to do, but the strategy wasn't executed properly. Was your tactical approach appropriate? On Facebook, did you investigate which posts were most popular, what posting times received the most engagement, or what should be posted based on EdgeRank? These are just some examples of how you could have been implementing your strategy to your best efforts and yet not implementing properly.

- **Are you investing too many resources?** You assumed that in order to execute, you needed x number of people or x budget. Did the people working on the program really spend as much time as you thought? Are you overinvested? Once again, this requires soul-searching and auditing to figure out what activities are taking up time without providing any social media benefits.

- **Were the assumptions in your social media strategy correct?** The strategy begins with objectives and assumptions, but given that social media is always in flux, things change. Maybe you assumed your target audience would be on one platform, but in the past six months they moved to another one. Reexamine assumptions and reevaluate at more frequent intervals if the maximum ROI wasn't achieved.

Maximizing social ROI relies on a number of factors, including having the right metrics to determine whether you achieved your business objective, tweaking the daily workflow (the D in PDCA), determining whether you had positive or negative ROI (the C in PDCA), and adjusting your strategy accordingly (the A in PDCA).

Chapter 18   Conclusion

The Future Evolution of Social Media and Your Social Media Strategy

This book was meant to provide you with a framework for cataloging your social media efforts and a strategy for documenting, planning, and implementing your social media strategy in such a way that you can best optimize your social media presence. It was also meant to offer targeted advice on how to cut through all the confusion and noise on the major social media platforms so that your company can maximize its social media presence on these specific platforms.

In the final chapters, we looked at the common issues that arise from companies implementing social media and how to help your company overcome them. We also covered problems with creating a social media strategy that isn't implementable, including issues such as staffing roles and responsibilities, and what you can do to ensure yours is. As we come to the end of this book, I encourage you to look forward and walk away with some advice on how things are going to change in the years to come—and how you can adjust your social media strategy accordingly.

PREDICTING THE FUTURE OF SOCIAL MEDIA . . . BY LOOKING AT ITS PAST

In Chapter 2, I discussed the ever-changing spectrum of social media—who uses these platforms, why we use them, and how the functionality of these platforms is constantly changing. Looking at past popular platforms, the one predictable thing you can walk away with is that social media is, for the most part, unpredictable. Despite social media's versatility, there are a few conclusions we can draw from current trends:

1. **These platforms are always changing.** Just as Google changes its search results algorithm, Facebook changes its EdgeRank algorithm regularly. There also appear to be similar algorithms at play in what appears in news feed updates on Twitter, LinkedIn, and Google+. These feeds want to show you popular posts in order to provide engaging content and reasons to stay on the platform as well as sponsored posts to help generate revenues.

2. **These platforms will continue to try to monetize their services through paid social.** Throughout this book I noted that paid social isn't necessarily a bad thing; it actually allows us to become more effective in amplifying our messaging and allowing our posts to be discovered. In representing a company, you should consider how you can best leverage these opportunities. However, if the big sites don't manage monetization correctly, it could affect these platforms as well as the performance of your ads. Just as we're always interested in optimizing how we perform on our own platforms by looking at metrics, we should always consider the effectiveness of the cost with the offerings available on these platforms.

3. **There will be an increasing shift to mobile, including smartphones as well as tablets, as their functionality and network speeds will only increase.** What you need to think about right now is whether your company's website is optimized for the mobile market. If people

are reaching your website through a mobile device, are they able to effectively and efficiently interact with it? To answer that question, check your website from a variety of devices, including iPhones, tablets, and Android phones. On a mobile site, things are laid out and function differently than on a web browser. You'll need to optimize your site so that it easily functions regardless of how people access it. If you're curious about the number of people arriving at your site using a mobile device, take a look at your Google Analytics; how do mobile visitors vary from desktop ones? Similarly, if you haven't placed an emphasis on it yet, being able to optimize your social media presence for mobile is going to be very important in the near future. Which platforms are most accessed by mobile? What do news feeds from the various sites look like on mobile? Which paid social elements can you leverage for mobile? Finally, there may come a point where it makes sense to repurpose some of your content into a mobile app above and beyond your website.

OUR INFATUATION WITH NEW SOCIAL MEDIA PLATFORMS

Clearly Facebook, Google+, Twitter, Instagram, YouTube, and Pinterest are major social media platforms right now, but there are always new sites on the horizon tempting us to spend time researching and learning how to tie these into our social media strategy mix. Twitter recently launched a new service called Vine,[1] which allows users to upload very short videos from a smartphone. In Japan, there's a new mobile communication platform called Line,[2] which has quickly amassed more than 100 million users. Quora and SlideShare are two others that are dancing on the edge of the social media playground, waiting to see if they'll be able to play with the big kids.

How can you deal with the constant introduction of these new platforms?

First, you can become an innovative experimenter. The second largest convenience store in Japan, Lawson,[3] is one such example. I recently had the good fortune of meeting the founder of the company's social media program, Akiko Shirai,[4] when I was in Tokyo. Lawson began its program because its Harvard-graduated chief executive officer (CEO) said back in February of 2010 that they needed to be constantly innovating in their approach to marketing and that social media had to play a part in this.

SOCIAL MEDIA REQUIRES CONSTANT INNOVATION, BY AKIKO SHIRAI

The message from the brand now is that it is always going to be experimenting with any new platform and figuring out how to incorporate it into the company strategy. Many companies aren't like that, instead looking only to optimize the limited resources they already have. Assuming only a small percentage of companies choose to be early innovators, what opportunities will they be able to grasp that many others will miss?

The results of the experiments that Lawson has periodically done in social media are impressive:

- The animated character Akiko-chan that Lawson created to represent itself in social media had the highest awareness level of any brand character, at 20 percent of those surveyed according to one survey.[5]
- The company's Mysterious Fried Chicken campaign, where "clues" were posted throughout social media, generated 6,257 retweets,[6] but more important, the amount of online traffic generated contributed to make the fried chicken its second best-selling product in company history.
- Lawson used Facebook Offers to offer a coupon for a 60-yen (approximately $0.60 in the United States) product that received a whopping 14 percent redemption rate, several times higher than its average of 3 percent. Seventy percent of those who redeemed from Facebook ended up spending an additional 368 yen, or more than $3.50, on other products, which led to a return on investment (ROI) worth more than seven times the company's initial investment.[7]
- Lawson now reaches more than 7.6 million fans on 22 different social media platforms—all while social media still represents less than 10 percent of its online marketing budget.

It is this embracing of never-ending experimentation and innovation that undoubtedly helped Lawson become the leading company in terms of sales from social media activity according to Nikkei BP.[8]

Akiko Shirai is manager of advertising and sales promotion for the Japanese convenience store franchise chain Lawson, which operates more than 10,000 stores in Japan, China, Indonesia, Thailand, and the United States.[9]

Back in the United States, I found another company with a similar story.

THE VALUE OF NEVER-ENDING SOCIAL MEDIA EXPERIMENTATION, BY JIM WENDT

Less than 16 months after entering the social media realm, Big Train leapfrogged past its direct competitors in terms of social media presence and engagement. In addition to significant on-page search engine optimization (SEO) efforts, social media and blog posts contributed to organic rankings lift in search engines. As of this writing, if you google for "drink mix manufacturer," the first three results are for Big Train.

Was it a coincidence that Big Train had its best performance in company history in 2012? Competition was watching and the biggest companies in the food and beverage world took notice. In late December 2012, Big Train was acquired by Kerry Inc., a global food and beverage powerhouse with more than $7.7 billion in revenues according to Hoovers.

Why did Kerry acquire Big Train? In addition to its great products and insanely loyal customers, Robyn Hawkins, Big Train's CEO at the time of the acquisition, said, "Developing and implementing a solid, aggressive, social media and Internet strategy definitely helped us grow our sales and profits, and played an important role in the acquisition." Embracing never-ending experimentation and innovation undoubtedly helped Big Train attract a strategic buyer.

Jim Wendt[10] is marketing manager of e-commerce and social media for the beverage manufacturer Big Train.[11]

If your company isn't necessarily seeking to be innovative, you can also take a wait and see approach or what I call the social media in the here and now approach. At the end of the day, you're never too late for social media. I signed up for Twitter in November 2008, thinking I was going to be way too late to truly take advantage of what it had to offer. In the spring of 2013, I attended the Social Media Marketing World conference in San Diego, where I had the opportunity to meet members of the Diners Club social media team, who confided in me that their company was relatively new to social media. Despite the fact that this global brand wasn't an early adopter, it still jumped in and is quickly making great strides in its social media marketing. At the conference, Diners Club made a splash by interviewing a number of the speakers and uploading the content to YouTube to provide social media advice for its members. One of these videos has already generated new brand awareness worth almost one-third of the total video views for its channel.[12]

If your company can't do it all (and most of them can't), use the platforms that work well for your situation and don't spend time on ones that aren't doing well. Be where your audience is, analyze your users and their habits, and learn what works best for your company. If you don't know if something is worth your company's time, give a new platform a try for three months or so as an experiment and see how it goes, but don't waste too much time on a site that isn't working. Don't go all in until there is a true ROI and added value for investing time, energy, and money into a particular social media platform.

THINGS ARE NEVER STATIC, EVEN ON OLD SOCIAL MEDIA PLATFORMS

We are a society that always jumps into the next big thing, and social media platforms are no exception. Sometimes sticking with a familiar platform while adjusting the strategy is the best way to manage social media marketing. Some platforms are nearly 10 years old, but just because they're older than others, it doesn't mean you shouldn't be experimenting and trying new things with the platform. Examine the different ways new users are using each of these platforms. Stay on top of updates being made to the social sites on which your company is active. New functionality is always being provided on social platforms; during your monthly or quarterly review, take a step back and assess what's working and how you can effectively change with the times. LinkedIn,[13] Twitter,[14] and Facebook[15] all have blogs where they post updates; throw these blogs in your RSS feed to allow you to track how things are changing. Social media isn't static, and there is always room for improvement when it comes to maximizing social.

With advice on creating and executing a social media strategy in hand and a look into the future of this online and mobile world, I hope you feel prepared to venture into this ever-evolving yet essential business space. There are no guarantees when it comes to social media, but if you continue to experiment, evaluate, analyze, and change your strategy as needed, your business will be able to maximize its social media ROI and create a road map that can be used to guide social media successfully throughout your entire company.

Thank you and good luck. Following my advice in this book, I hope to include the case study of your successful social media usage in my next book.

Notes

INTRODUCTION

1. http://maximizesocialbusiness.com/social-media-stragety-top-marketer
   -questions-8757/.

CHAPTER 1   REALITY CHECK: THE PERMEATING TRENDS OF SOCIAL
   MEDIA AND SOCIAL BUSINESS

1. http://twitpic.com/135xa.
2. www.editorsweblog.org/2009/01/19/twitter-first-off-the-mark-with
   -hudson-plane-crash-coverage.
3. www.mediabistro.com/fishbowlny/nyt-covers-the-hudson-river-plane-
   crash_b10882.
4. venturebeat.com/2013/03/14/japans-line-mobile-messaging-app-reaches-
   100m-game-downloads/.
5. www.sec.gov/news/press/2013/2013-51.htm.

CHAPTER 2   A SOCIAL MEDIA STRATEGY: THE FRAMEWORK FOR THE EVER-CHANGING WORLD OF SOCIAL MEDIA

1. www.europeanbusinessreview.com/?p=6529.
2. According to Facebook ads demographic data on April 5, 2013.
3. http://en.wikipedia.org/wiki/Twitter.
4. http://mashable.com/2012/02/12/whitney-houston-twitter/.
5. http://ibrahimhasan.com/content/brief-history-linkedin.
6. http://en.wikipedia.org/wiki/PDCA.
7. http://en.wikipedia.org/wiki/W._Edwards_Deming.

CHAPTER 3   DETERMINING OBJECTIVES AND BACKGROUND FOR YOUR SOCIAL MEDIA PROGRAM

1. www.compete.com.
2. www.alexa.com.
3. www.google.com/adplanner.
4. http://support.google.com/youtube/bin/answer.py?hl=en&answer=71673.

CHAPTER 4   AUDITING YOUR SOCIAL MEDIA PROGRAM

1. http://en.wikipedia.org/wiki/PDCA.
2. http://maximizesocialbusiness.com/i-blog-for-content-not-for-comments-surprised-6510/.
3. www.klout.com, www.peerindex.com, and www.kred.com, respectively.

CHAPTER 5   CORE ELEMENTS AND CONCEPTS IN YOUR SOCIAL MEDIA STRATEGY

1. http://en.wikipedia.org/wiki/Flesch%E2%80%93Kincaid_readability_test%23Flesch_Reading_Ease.
2. www.feedly.com.
3. www.netvibes.com.
4. www.newsblur.com.
5. www.theoldreader.com.
6. http://en.wikipedia.org/wiki/Inbound_marketing.
7. www.inqbation.com/most-popular-cms-on-the-internet/.
8. www.slashgear.com/tumblr-boasts-nearly-170-million-monthly-visitors-27258434/.

9. www.comscore.com/Insights/Blog/Tumblr_Defies_its_Name_as_
   User_Growth_Accelerates.
10. www.huffingtonpost.com/2012/10/04/facebook-1-billion-users_n_
    1938675.html.
11. According to Alexa.com statistics on April 14, 2013.
12. www.businessinsider.com/facebook-wins-in-social-media-time
    -spend-2013-3.
13. www.usatoday.com/story/money/business/2013/03/09/10-web
    -sites-most-visited/1970835/.
14. http://techcrunch.com/2012/07/31/twitter-may-have-500m-users-but
    -only-170m-are-active-75-on-twitters-own-clients/.
15. www.forbes.com/sites/tjmccue/2013/01/29/twitter-ranked-fastest
    -growing-social-platform-in-the-world/.
16. http://blog.linkedin.com/2013/01/09/linkedin-200-million/.
17. www.scriptiny.com/2013/01/525-million-google-plus-accounts-as
    -of-january-2013/.
18. www.forbes.com/sites/anthonykosner/2013/01/26/watch-out-face
    book-with-google-at-2-and-youtube-at-3-google-inc-could-catch-up/.
19. http://marketingland.com/if-googles-really-proud-of-google-it-should
    -share-some-real-user-figures-9796.
20. http://youtube-global.blogspot.com/2013/03/onebillionstrong.html.
21. www.jeffbullas.com/2013/02/11/the-facts-and-figures-on-youtube
    -in-2013-infographic/.
22. http://techcrunch.com/2012/02/07/pinterest-monthly-uniques/.
23. http://en.wikipedia.org/wiki/Pinterest.
24. www.thestorestarters.com/10-pinterest-statistics-you-cant-ignore
    -for-your-new-store/.
25. http://techcrunch.com/2012/09/06/report-pinterest-beats-yahoo-organic
    -traffic-making-it-4th-largest-traffic-driver-worldwide/.
26. http://blog.instagram.com/post/44078783561/100-million.
27. www.big-boards.com/.
28. http://techcrunch.com/2013/01/10/diggs-users-doubled-since-august
    -monetization-efforts-continue/.
29. http://mashable.com/2012/10/31/reddit-valuation/.
30. http://mashable.com/2012/04/26/stumbleupon-hits-25-million-users-and
    -is-gaining-1-million-a-month/.
31. http://news.cnet.com/8301-1023_3-57573689-93/linkedin-pitches
    -slideshare-as-advertising/.
32. http://gigaom.com/2012/10/01/how-foursquare-is-building-a-revenue
    -strategy-around-local-search/.
33. http://searchengineland.com/yelp-posts-q2-revenue-gain-claims-78
    -million-users-globally-129292.
34. www.theverge.com/2013/3/20/4121574/flickr-chief-markus
    -spiering-talks-photos-and-marissa-mayer.

35. www.guardian.co.uk/technology/appsblog/2013/may/21/flickr-1tb-storage-android-app.

36. http://royal.pingdom.com/2013/01/16/internet-2012-in-numbers/.

37. http://stateofthemedia.org/2012/audio-how-far-will-digital-go/audio-by-the-numbers/.

38. http://allthingsd.com/20130104/six-podcasting-predictions-for-2013/.

39. www.worldwidewebsize.com/.

40. http://blog.hubspot.com/blog/tabid/6307/bid/34080/Why-Marketers-Need-to-Rise-Above-the-Deluge-of-Crappy-Content.aspx.

41. http://techcrunch.com/2012/01/17/how-often-should-facebook-pages-post/.

42. It should be noted that although LinkedIn has never formally announced an EdgeRank type of algorithm for its news feed, it is clear from my user experience that there is some type of filtering occurring.

43. http://landing.conversocial.com/report-a-day-in-the-life-of-brands-on-twitter.

CHAPTER 6   BLOGGING AS AN ESSENTIAL PART OF EVERY SOCIAL MEDIA STRATEGY

1. www.umassd.edu/cmr/socialmedia/2012fortune500/.

2. www.medialifemagazine.com/huh-online-nearly-equals-tv-in-daily-usage/.

3. www.mindjumpers.com/blog/2012/05/time-spend-online/.

4. For a definition and explanation of social signals and how they affect SEO, read http://blog.leadingwsiwebsolutions.com/2013/04/seo-relevancy-social-signals-whats-your-strategy/.

5. http://blog.hubspot.com/blog/tabid/6307/bid/5014/Study-Shows-Business-Blogging-Leads-to-55-More-Website-Visitors.aspx.

6. http://trends.builtwith.com/cms.

CHAPTER 7   MAXIMIZING YOUR FACEBOOK PRESENCE

1. www.pewinternet.org/Reports/2011/Technology-and-social-networks/Part-3/SNS-users.aspx.

2. http://socialfresh.com/facebook-newsfeed-time-spent/.

3. http://simplymeasured.com/blog/2012/03/27/the-impact-of-facebook-timeline-for-brands-study/.

4. www.michaelleander.me/blog/facebook-engagement-tactics-the-lifetime-of-a-post-on-a-facebook-page/.

5. www.edgerankchecker.com.
6. www.huffingtonpost.com/2012/02/29/facebook-posts_n_1311330.html.
7. www.postplanner.com.
8. www.marketingcharts.com/wp/interactive/us-facebook-ad-cpcs-rose-during-h2-2012-26147/.
9. www.seomoz.org/blog/5-killer-seo-insights-from-analyzing-a-billion-dollars-in-adwords-spend.
10. http://en.community.dell.com/dell-groups/sbc/b/weblog/archive/2012/10/01/facebook-ads-tips-amp-best-practices-for-better-ad-performance.aspx.
11. www.searchenginejournal.com/facebook-marketing-roi-3-case-studies/28254/.
12. www.businessinsider.com/facebook-reveals-how-samsung-turned-a-10-million-ad-buy-to-129-in-sales-2012-11.
13. http://socialfresh.com/facebook-advertising-examples/.
14. www.facebook.com/page_guidelines.php.

CHAPTER 8   MAXIMIZING YOUR TWITTER PRESENCE

1. http://socialmediatoday.com/mlewis1/913846/state-social-marketing-survey-infographic.
2. www.slideshare.net/PingElizabeth/the-state-of-social-media-marketing-report-awarenessinc.
3. http://therealtimereport.com/2011/03/18/77-of-fortune-global-100-companies-use-twitter/.
4. http://cdn2.hubspot.net/hub/53/blog/docs/ebooks/120-marketing-stats-charts-and-graphs.pdf.
5. www.businessinsider.com/twitter-search-is-bigger-than-bing-and-yahoo-search-combined-2010-4.
6. http://maximizesocialbusiness.com/top-25-twitter-clients-top-50-social-media-influencers-9349/.
7. www.feedly.com.
8. http://tippingpointlabs.com/2009/07/01/twitter-is-dead-long-live-twitter/.
9. http://blog.marketo.com/blog/2012/07/the-4-1-1-rule-for-lead-nurturing.html.
10. http://bit.ly/TwitterChatMaster.
11. http://maximizesocialbusiness.com/what-is-twitter-chat-tweetgrid-2175/.
12. http://maximizesocialbusiness.com/twitter-chat-best-practices-dun-and-broadstreet-8460/.
13. www.linkedin.com/in/shellylucas.
14. https://business.twitter.com/success-stories/optify.

CHAPTER 9   MAXIMIZING YOUR LINKEDIN PRESENCE

1. http://online360.ekobuzz.com/5-ways-to-use-linkedin-to-boost-your-online-marketing/.
2. http://cdn2.hubspot.net/hub/53/blog/docs/ebooks/the_2012_state_of_inbound_marketing.pdf.
3. http://blog.hubspot.com/blog/tabid/6307/bid/30030/LinkedIn-277-More-Effective-for-Lead-Generation-Than-Facebook-Twitter-New-Data.aspx.
4. http://press.linkedin.com/about.
5. http://wind.mn/linksalesbook.
6. http://press.linkedin.com/about.
7. www.linkedin.com/groups?gid=1976445.
8. http://cn.linkedin.com/in/globaltrading.
9. www.linkedin.com/in/lanettehanson/.
10. www.linkedin.com/groups/California-Workers-Compensation-Risk-Conference-1911180.
11. www.linkedin.com/groups?gid=2308956.
12. http://marketing.linkedin.com/sites/default/files/pdfs/LinkedIn_Philips CaseStudy2011.pdf.
13. http://marketing.linkedin.com/sites/default/files/pdfs/LinkedIn_Chevron CaseStudy2011.pdf.
14. http://marketing.linkedin.com/sites/default/files/pdfs/LinkedIn_HPUK CaseStudy2011.pdf.
15. www.linkedin.com/company/hewlett-packard.
16. http://marketing.linkedin.com/sites/default/files/pdfs/LinkedIn_VWIndia_CaseStudy2011.pdf.

CHAPTER 10   MAXIMIZING YOUR GOOGLE+ PRESENCE

1. http://googleblog.blogspot.com/2012/01/search-plus-your-world.html.
2. http://econsultancy.com/us/blog/9972-how-does-google-impact-seo-performance.
3. http://en.wikipedia.org/wiki/PageRank.
4. www.searchmetrics.com/en/services/ranking-factors-2013.
5. https://plus.google.com/+MarkTraphagen.
6. http://gigaom.com/2011/07/18/dell-google-hangouts/.
7. www.socialmediaexaminer.com/businesses-using-google-hangouts/.
8. www.google.com/+/learnmore/hangouts/onair.html.
9. http://maximizesocialbusiness.com/google-plus-communities-connect-your-brand-7677/.
10. http://news.cnet.com/8301-1023_3-57514241-93/google-signs-up-400-million-users-with-100-million-active/.

11. www.seomoz.org/blog/your-guide-to-social-signals-for-seo.
12. www.virante.com/blog/2012/01/08/how-to-show-your-author
    -photo-in-google-search-results/.
13. www.virante.org/blog/2011/11/15/how-to-verify-your-google
    -brand-page-with-google/.
14. http://maximizesocialbusiness.com/author/mark-traphagen.
15. www.virante.com/blog.

CHAPTER 11   MAXIMIZING VISUAL SOCIAL NETWORKS

1. http://contentmarketinginstitute.com.
2. http://contentmarketinginstitute.com/2012/12/social-media-content
   -marketing-predictions-2013/.
3. Doug Rushkoff, *Present Shock* (New York: Penguin Group, 2013).
4. www.clickz.com/clickz/column/2120986/brain-website-selling.
5. http://techcrunch.com/2012/09/06/report-pinterest-beats-yahoo-organic
   -traffic-making-it-4th-largest-traffic-driver-worldwide/.
6. http://maximizesocialbusiness.com/pinterest-security-risks-6555/.
7. http://maximizesocialbusiness.com/author/bob-geller/.
8. www.fusionpr.com/.
9. www.warrencass.com/social-media-case-study-blendtec-and-youtube/.
10. www.vizioninteractive.com/blog/youtube-case-study-how-orabrush
    -got-into-wal-mart-and-top-three-strategies-you-should-take-away/.
11. www.slideshare.net/MLNL/gillette-a-youtube-case-study.
12. www.youtube.com/yt/press/statistics.html.
13. www.jeffbullas.com/2012/05/23/35-mind-numbing-youtube-facts
    -figures-and-statistics-infographic/.
14. http://support.google.com/youtube/bin/answer.py?hl=en&answer=2781780.
15. www.forbes.com/forbesinsights/video_in_the_csuite/.
16. http://maximizesocialbusiness.com/social-media-platforms/youtube/.
17. http://beta.abc.go.com/shows/americas-funniest-home-videos.
18. http://wearesocial.net/blog/2010/08/wieden-kennedys-spice-case-study/.
19. http://maximizesocialbusiness.com/give-social-media-campaign-face-with
    -video-6675/.
20. http://maximizesocialbusiness.com/author/jayson-duncan/.
21. www.millerfarmmedia.com/.
22. According to www.alexa.com.
23. www.mediabistro.com/alltwitter/usa-social-network-use_b18798.
24. http://searchengineland.com/pinterest-now-sending-more-traffic-than
    -yahoo-search-shareaholic-says-132329.
25. http://sproutsocial.com/insights/2012/05/pinterest-e-commerce-study/.
26. www.gigya.com/case-studies/indigo/.

27. www.socialmediaexaminer.com/pinterest-case-study-sony/.
28. www.inc.com/marla-tabaka/why-pinterest-should-matter-to-you.html.
29. www.richrelevance.com/blog/2012/09/social-infographic/.
30. http://venturebeat.com/2013/02/27/sephora-our-pinterest-followers
    -spend-15x-more-than-our-facebook-followers/.
31. www.marketingprofs.com/charts/2013/10139/social-network
    -demographics-twitter-pinterest-instagram-facebook.
32. http://blog.rjmetrics.com/pinterest-data-analysis-an-inside-look/.
33. http://pinleague.com/pinterest-contest-guidelines/.
34. http://business.pinterest.com/logos-and-marketing-guidelines/.
35. http://news.cnet.com/8301-1023_3-57412142-93/instagram-users-are
    -young-and-facebook-users-are-old/.
36. http://instagram.com/shopexcessbaggage.
37. http://mashable.com/2012/07/03/instagram-for-business/.
38. http://help.instagram.com/454502981253053/.
39. http://allfacebook.com/simply-measured-instagram-study_b111108.

CHAPTER 12   DETERMINING STAFFING ROLES AND RESPONSIBILITIES

1. http://socialmediatoday.com/SMC/104490.
2. http://econsultancy.com/us/blog/7913-14-epic-social-media-fails.
3. http://growyourbusinessblog.com/interns-gone-wild-five-social-media
   -blunders/.
4. http://maximizesocialbusiness.com/all-nippon-airways-facebook-content
   -stragety-8493/.
5. www.slideshare.net/Altimeter/the-evolution-of-social-business-six
   -stages-of-social-media-transformation.
6. www.slideshare.net/Altimeter/the-evolution-of-social-business-six
   -stages-of-social-media-transformation.
7. www.web-strategist.com/blog/2010/11/09/research-most-companies
   -organize-in-hub-and-spoke-formation/.
8. www.web-strategist.com/blog/2011/04/04/program-plan-the
   -social-media-center-of-excellence/.
9. http://twitter.com/coryedwards.

CHAPTER 13   ONBOARDING YOUR SOCIAL MEDIA STRATEGY

1. www.dragonflyeffect.com/blog/?page_id=1380.
2. www.proskauer.com/news/press-releases/november-14-2012/proskauer-
   study-recommends-corporate-best-practices-for-navigating-challenges-of-
   social-media-use-in-the-workplace/.

3. www.olympic.org/Documents/Games_London_2012/IOC_Social_Media_Blogging_and_Internet_Guidelines-London.pdf.

4. http://stream.wsj.com/story/london-olympics-2012/SS-2-13789/SS-2-34508/.

5. www.marketingprofs.com/events/May_2010/files/b2b0510_social_media_guidelines.pdf.

6. http://maximizesocialbusiness.com/author/joel-don/.

7. www.commstrategies.com/.

8. www.isa.org/.

9. http://wind.mn/17yahHA.

10. http://maximizesocialbusiness.com/enterprise-social-networks-internal-communication-8106/.

11. www.ioic.org.uk/content/latest-news/2303-coty2012.html.

12. http://maximizesocialbusiness.com/author/rachel-miller/.

13. http://allthingsic.com/.

CHAPTER 14   MANAGING THE RISKS

1. www.umassd.edu/cmr/studiesandresearch/2012inc500socialmedia update/.

2. http://money.cnn.com/2011/02/03/news/companies/KennethCole_twitter/index.htm?iid=EL.

3. http://money.cnn.com/galleries/2011/technology/1104/gallery.social_media_controversies/6.html.

4. http://money.cnn.com/galleries/2011/technology/1104/gallery.social_media_controversies/3.html.

5. http://econsultancy.com/us/blog/11056-the-top-10-social-media-fails-of-2012.

6. www.ediscoverylawalert.com/uploads/file/IN%20Re%20NTL.pdf.

7. www.cmswire.com/cms/customer-experience/social-media-mixes-with-financial-industry-014903.php.

8. http://rlstollar.wordpress.com/2013/02/02/applebees-overnight-social-media-meltdown-a-photo-essay/.

9. www.sayitsocial.com/blog/2013/02/3-ways-nascar-failed-with-social-media-crisis-pr-and-how-they-could-have-prevented-it/.

10. http://scholar.google.com/scholar_case?case=16227806786911947872&hl=en&as_sdt=2&as_vis=1&oi=scholarr.

11. www.phonedog.com.

12. https://twitter.com/noahkravitz.

13. http://thenextweb.com/twitter/2011/12/27/can-you-own-your-twitter-followers-one-blog-seems-to-think-so/.

14. http://thenextweb.com/socialmedia/2012/02/02/phonedog-vs-noah-kravitz-the-twitter-case-continues/.

15. http://management.fortune.cnn.com/2012/12/13/twitter-work-employees/.
16. Disclaimer: Information provided in this book is not legal advice, nor should you act on anything stated in this article without conferring with this contributor or other legal counsel regarding your specific situation.
17. For additional information about employee workplace privacy, or lack of privacy, and for analysis of a recent US Supreme Court decision on the privacy of employee texts, see http://windmillnetworking.com/2012/07/03/social-media-privacy-in-the-workplace-is-there-any/.
18. http://law.onecle.com/california/labor/232.html.
19. www.dol.gov/whd/overtime_pay.htm.
20. www.cnn.com/2012/02/07/tech/social-media/companies-social-media/index.html.
21. http://en.wikipedia.org/wiki/At-will_employment.
22. http://maximizesocialbusiness.com/author/james-wu/.
23. www.jameswulaw.com/.
24. http://en.wikipedia.org/wiki/United_Breaks_Guitarsn.
25. http://blog.jetblue.com/index.php/2011/10/31/a-note-from-our-coo/.
26. http://maximizesocialbusiness.com/author/christopher-budd/.
27. www.christopherbudd.com/.

CHAPTER 15   CREATING YOUR PDCA WORKFLOW

1. Some samples and advice on social media content calendar creation can be found here: www.toprankblog.com/2012/10/winning-content-types/, http://blog.hubspot.com/blog/tabid/6307/bid/33415/The-Social-Media-Publishing-Schedule-Every-Marketer-Needs-Template.aspx, and http://digitalsherpa.com/using-a-content-calendar-to-manage-your-social-media-presence/.
2. http://twitter.com/JasonEng.
3. http://twitter.com/SonyProUSA.

CHAPTER 16   INTEGRATING YOUR SOCIAL MEDIA STRATEGY

1. www.emarketer.com/Article/How-Smartphone-PC-Internet-Users-Different/1009589.
2. http://econsultancy.com/us/blog/11186-will-mobile-internet-replace-desktop-infographic.
3. www.google.com/think/research-studies/creating-moments-that-matter.html.
4. http://searchengineland.com/study-43-percent-of-total-google-search-queries-have-local-intent-135428.

5. www.strategicdriven.com/marketing-insights-blog/Brand -Ambassadors-Employee-Program-Amplifies-Corporate-Culture/.

6. http://maximizesocialbusiness.com/building-social-into-marketing -competitive-advantage-6752/.

7. www.brandchannel.com/home/post/2011/07/15/Economist-EIU -Social-Commerce-Report.aspx.

8. http://maximizesocialbusiness.com/author/joe-ruiz/.

9. www.strategicdriven.com/.

10. http://techcrunch.com/2012/08/22/how-big-is-facebooks-data-2-5-billion -pieces-of-content-and-500-terabytes-ingested-every-day/.

11. www.womma.org/blog/2013/02/the-marketers-guide-to -social-customer-data-by-shoutlet.

12. http://instagram.com/press/.

13. www.mediabistro.com/alltwitter/social-media-stats-2012_b30651.

14. www.youtube.com/yt/press/statistics.html.

15. www.magazine.pamplin.vt.edu/fall12/vehicledefects.html.

16. www.hypebot.com/hypebot/2012/12/data-science-and-the-music -industry-what-social-media-has-to-do-with-record-sales.html.

17. www.slideshare.net/dhinchcliffe/asae-tech-conference -2012-closing-keynote-on-disruptive-tech.

18. www.ft.com/cms/s/0/bd5a5ce2-aa57-11e1-899d-00144feabdc0 .html#axzz2QnExwYeA.

19. www.slideshare.net/scribesoft/cmo-imperative-convergence-2013.

20. http://www2.mzinga.com/survey2012.

21. http://en.wikipedia.org/wiki/Social_CRM.

22. www.marketingcharts.com/wp/direct/social-crm-adoption -seen-low-but-expected-to-grow-23363/.

CHAPTER 17   THE ROI OF YOUR SOCIAL MEDIA STRATEGY

1. www.wired.com/insights/2013/04/the-state-of-social-sharing -in-2013-infographic/.

2. www.chrisbrogan.com/the-passion-of-gary-vaynerchuk/.

3. https://twitter.com/garyvee/status/208994579331035139.

CHAPTER 18   CONCLUSION: THE FUTURE EVOLUTION OF SOCIAL MEDIA AND YOUR SOCIAL MEDIA STRATEGY

1. http://blog.twitter.com/2013/01/vine-new-way-to-share-video.html.

2. http://techcrunch.com/2013/03/17/line-the-social-entertainment-platform/.

3. http://en.wikipedia.org/wiki/Lawson_(store).
4. http://toyokeizai.net/articles/-/11155.
5. http://gaiax-socialmedialab.jp/line/195.
6. www.wab.ne.jp/wab_sites/contents/1629.
7. http://prezi.com/uru2o4xvu8wo/about-lawsoninc/.
8. http://corporate.nikkeibp.co.jp/information/newsrelease/newsrelease 20130222.shtml.
9. http://lawson.jp/en/.
10. www.jimmywendt.com.
11. www.bigtrain.com.
12. www.youtube.com/playlist?list=PL8xyoHKe7jpUZeOSzxXvU7gH_7H9 OqK6u.
13. http://blog.linkedin.com/.
14. http://blog.twitter.com/.
15. http://blog.facebook.com/.

Acknowledgments

I am grateful every day for those around me who support, educate, and inspire me to do things I never thought possible. It was 4½ years ago when my wife first suggested I write a book, and here I am completing my third one in that relatively short time. It is impossible to thank everyone who has helped me along the way, but allow me to thank those extra special people in my life.

MY FAMILY

My wife, Miwako, and children, Luna and Kyle, have been as supportive as a family can be while Daddy was busy writing. If not for them, I simply would not have found the time to write this book with the crazy work schedule that I have. My parents continue to support in me all of my endeavors, and all of my brothers and their extended families have offered me advice that has helped form the person who I am.

THE MAN WHO MADE THIS BOOK HAPPEN

An OpenLink message on LinkedIn from sales guru and now fellow John Wiley & Sons, Inc., author Art Sobczak was the spark that eventually led me to an introduction to this great publisher. Thank you, Art, for being a fan of *Maximizing LinkedIn for Sales and Social Media Marketing*— and for taking the initiative to help connect the dots. This book literally would not have happened if not for your reaching out to me.

MY PUBLISHING TEAM

My production team at John Wiley & Sons, Inc., which includes Lauren Murphy, Susan Moran, Lydia Dimitriadis, Maureen Drexel, and Adrianna Johnson, have been the most incredible people to work with, providing me guidance when necessary and trust in my writing. JoAnna Haguen, who edited my previous book, also played a large role in helping me craft my words for this book, for which I am indebted. Maximize Social Business contributors Debbie Miller and Courtney Ramirez additionally helped me with my writing and deserve my gratitude for the assistance they offered.

MY MAXIMIZE SOCIAL BUSINESS BLOGGERS AND CONTRIBUTORS TO THIS BOOK

All of my Maximize Social Business bloggers deserve a very special thank you for putting their trust in me and collaborating together in building a social media for business resource. Some of you provided contributions that further increase the value that this book will have for every reader. Regardless of whether you are a part of this book or not, I want you to know that I thank both past and present contributors Amy Stephan, Judy Gombita, Craig Jamieson, Bob Geller, Joseph Ruiz, Jessica Rogers, Lilach Bullock, Christopher Budd, Jayson Duncan, James Wu, Mark Traphagen, Raymond Morin, Joel Don, Deborah Anne Gibbs, Rebekah Radice, Joellyn Sargent, Tony Restell, Claire Axelrad, Alex Kutsishin, Aaron Lee, Tammy Kahn Fennell, Kristi Hines, Rachel Miller, Chris Treadway, Dean Soto, Kyle-Beth Hilfer, and Michelle Sherman.

MY READERS AND ONLINE NETWORK

I could not have come as far as I am today without you loyal readers of my previous two books, subscribers and commenters on my Maximize Social Business (or previous Windmill Networking) blog, as well as those who have connected, followed, befriended, and circled me online. Your daily engagement is what provides me the energy and motivation to continue being who I am and doing what I do in social media.

MY LOCAL FRIENDS

Although social media has made me slightly antisocial locally because of business travel, I am still indebted to those of you in Orange County, California, who continue to support me in social media, even if we don't see each other as often as we used to (in alphabetical order): Joel Don, Debbie Miller, Ted Nguyen, Dean Soto, Marcie Taylor, Paul Tran, Tim Tyrell-Smith, Rochelle Veturis, and Jim and MaryAnne Wendt.

MY CUSTOMERS

This book would not have been possible if not for all of the customers, large and small, who put their trust in me and gave me the opportunity to guide them on the creation and implementation of their social media strategy.

About the Author

Neal Schaffer is a trilingual social media strategy consultant, coach, and speaker. After nearly two decades of working in B2B sales, business development, and marketing helping companies successfully establish sales organizations from scratch in competitive Asian markets, Neal is currently the President of Windmills Marketing, where he has worked with dozens of companies on creating social media strategies, auditing and optimizing their current social media programs, and training employees from various departments on leveraging social media for business.

As a popular social media speaker, Neal has spoken at more than 150 events on three continents and regularly presents on social media in Japan, speaking in Japanese. He also teaches as part of the renowned Mini Social Media MBA program at Rutgers University.

In addition to writing *Maximizing LinkedIn for Sales and Social Media Marketing* and *Windmill Networking: Understanding, Leveraging and Maximizing LinkedIn*, Neal is also the creator of an AdAge Top 100

Global Marketing Blog, Windmill Networking (recently rebranded as Maximize Social Business), as well as the host of the popular weekly podcast *Social Business Unplugged*.

You can find Neal online at his digital gateway nealschaffer.com, his business site windmillnetworking.com, or his blog maximizesocial business.com. He is also on Twitter at @nealschaffer.

Index